NEW BUSINESS
BREAKTHROUGH
STRATEGIES

FOR

ACCOUNTANTS

HOW TO ATTRACT AND RETAIN YOUR IDEAL CLIENT

PETER LAWSON

www.newbusinessbreakthroughs.com. au

ISBN 10: 0987461346
ISBN 13: 9780987461346

TESTIMONIALS

If you are a professional in business, Peter does not tell you what you want to hear but what you need to hear. A great insight into how the rules have all changed, including lots of good case studies. I would recommend this as required reading for any professional considering starting a business, or for those professionals that want to grow their business.

Chris Ridd
Managing Director, Australia, Xero Accounting Software

Having worked as an adviser to and coach of professionals for thirty five years now, I have seen too many young ones buried in technical work without any introduction to how to win new clients and review their needs and negotiate a fixed fee for the role to be played as their adviser. In this book, Peter discusses the theory then backs it up with pragmatic case studies and real life tips. All Young Guns (as we call young professionals) should read and practice what is in this book. It will make a big difference to your career!

Andrew Geddes

Peter Lawson has the unprecedented ability to take complex business topics and make them simple, yet effective and profitable. Any accountant, regardless of their skill level, will find this book to be a windfall for their practice. A MUST read!

Adrian Ulsh
Author of the highly acclaimed book "How Small Business Owners Can Instantly Generate All The
Leads Their Business Can Handle... WITHOUT Spending A Dime On Marketing Or Advertising"

Another dynamic, enjoyable and insightful business book by Peter Lawson. He has an uncanny ability to take a complex business concept...and make it simple.

A must read for any accountant looking to take their practice to the next level.

Karl Bryan

DISCLAIMER

Copyright © 2014 Peter Lawson
All rights reserved

MARKETING PAGE

Other books written by Peter Lawson:-

Creative Cash Flow - 8 Innovative Business Strategies to Boost Profit

#1 Best Seller on Amazon
http://www.amazon.com/dp/B00ALLR84Y/ref=rdr_kindle_ext_tmb

WEBSITE TO CONNECT WITH YOU

www.newbusinessbreakthroughs.com.au

Self-Published - Peter Lawson

If you have any questions simply shoot me an email at:

peter@newbusinessbreakthroughs.com.au

DEDICATION

This book is dedicated to my darling wife Gina for her continual support and backup and for putting up with the early morning starts. She's been a shoulder to cry on and a mate to celebrate with.

Not just a wife... a friend for life.

ACKNOWLEDGMENTS

To the accounting profession and all those that are a part of the accounting community. You have the knowledge and expertise to help thousands of small business owners achieve that once in a lifetime dream...the dream of owning a million dollar business.

Proactive accountants need to be out there helping small business owners achieve their goals. Unfortunately, most accountants do not have the skills to communicate their range of skills to small business owners in order to have the opportunity to assist them to grow their business to this million dollar level.

And that is the reason why I decided to take a chunk out of my life and write this book. If I can provide some marketing strategies to accountants, and they can use these strategies to demonstrate their value to small business owners to assist them to grow their business...then my work is done.

I was fortunate to find two guys who I consider to be amongst the best marketers in the world... In fact, they are such great marketers, they found me.

Their names are Karl Bryan and Adrian Ulsh and I have to say, I have never met a more dedicated, passionate and hardworking pair of men in my life. They run a business called Leader Publishing Worldwide and they have given me the ability to assist my fellow accountants with the marketing expertise they need to attract quality clients to their practices.

By implementing their marketing system, my marketing skills improved ten-fold, and so did my business. I went from a virtual standing start to a six figure income in just under six months and I have Karl and Adrian to thank for that.

So, thanks guys, for providing me with the tools and resources to get more accountants in front of more small business owners.

CONTENTS

INTRODUCTION

Have you ever thought what it would be like to have your own accounting firm?

Were your dreams shattered when you thought about the capital that would be required (that you don't have) to set up the business? And then you started thinking about the cost of equipment, the office fit out, the hiring of personnel, and the fact that you have to pay living expenses while you are getting your practice off the ground.

If you are an entrepreneurial professional and want to fast-track the growth of your practice and boost profit; you have come to the right place. If you want to have fun doing this, you have also come to the right place. And for those ambitious professionals that are not yet qualified and just don't know how, or when, to set-up their own practice, then chapter one will demonstrate a proven strategy to help you get started.

Throughout this book you will learn proven strategies about how to build a successful and profitable accounting practice. I emphasise the word profit because most accounting firms, even though they experience growth, do not grow profit along with that growth. This book will demonstrate why that happens and you will find out how to avoid this common trap.

Accountants often fall into the trap of thinking that the more clients they have the more successful the practice. But it is not the quantity of clients, but the quality of clients that really will add the numbers to the bottom line. The strategies throughout this book will show you how to grow your client base, how to identify and retain your ideal clients.

For those smart, ambitious and entrepreneurial accountants I understand the frustrations and the challenges you face establishing your own Practice.

Let me explain...

When I was age 20 I had the same ambitious thoughts. I was a young trainee accountant and wanted my own show. I wanted to be in control of my own destiny and reap the benefits of my hard work. It was at this early stage that I decided I would start up a Professional Knowledge Firm of my own. And I was prepared to do whatever I had to do to get the business off the ground. When I started out I had no money, no clients and lacked knowledge, but I did have a strategy and a goal.

I started my own accounting practice at age 25 with only enough money to cover living expenses for the next two months. I also had some clients that I had accumulated whilst employed (I will tell you more about this in chapter one). The biggest thing going for me was the desire to achieve my goals. I did some advertising in the local newspaper and introduced myself to all the local business owners. I let everyone know that I now had my own accounting practice, which meant I could not turn back or give up.

In addition to that I worked my butt off, and in less than six months I put my shingle on a little office that I sub-let from a solicitor, who turned out to be a great referral source. The rest is ancient history.

This book is aimed at pro-active accountants that want to make a difference with their clients. Throughout the book I will run through some creative strategies that do not require enormous amounts of capital to implement. These strategies have proven to be successful through a lot of trial, error and continual tweaking. The same rule applies, you learn from mistakes. You can also learn from success because success leaves clues.

The main thing that an accountant needs in this day and age is good communication skills and the ability to gain rapport with people. Marketing, via social media and networking groups, is at your fingertips. One of the big advantages here is that this form of creative advertising will not burn a hole in your marketing budget.

So if you want to work *smart* and not *hard* and enjoy the lifestyle and benefits that come from owning a successful accounting practice, this book will give you some strategies that will help you along the way. The book has some great start-up strategies in chapter one. In the remaining chapters there are strategies for established professionals who are looking for ideas about how to grow their business and boost profits. There are chapters devoted to marketing and growing your practice with outside-the-box ideas.

In the nine chapters that follow, you will learn some strategies that I found most useful in establishing and growing my own accounting practice, along with skills I have learnt from fellow practitioners over the years.

Throughout the book there will be a number of case studies and I highly recommend that you use these and the examples and action steps so you learn from my experiences and the experiences of other successful professionals that I've worked with over the years.

The biggest risk you will ever take in business is not taking a risk at all. You don't want to die guessing or wondering how things would have turned out had you not taken that first small leap of faith. In order to achieve you need to have faith in your greatest asset...YOU.

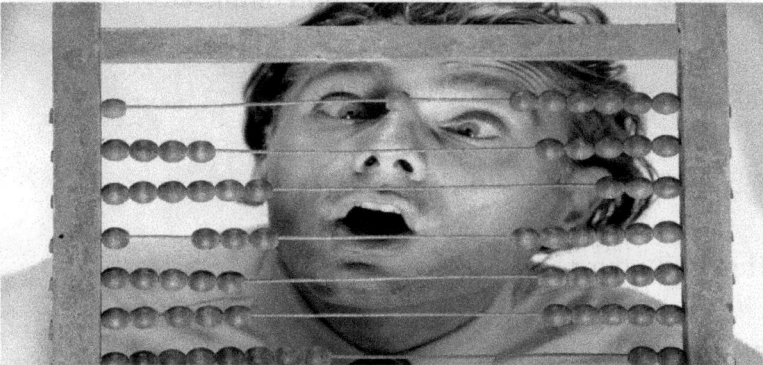

I have just one favour to ask. When you have finished reading this book, select two strategies and implement them in the next 90 days. As a minimum gain some feedback from your clients (and prospective clients) by conducting a Client Engagement Review (CER) as referred to in chapter 6. You will be amazed at the results.

In each chapter you will learn:
- The Strategy
- The Step-By-Step Process
- How it Works
- Why it Works
- The Benefits
- Case Studies
- Action Steps to Assist With the Implementation of these Strategies
- Recommended Resources.

If at the end of this book, you feel you have some questions you would like to ask, or you would like to connect with me and learn more, please visit the website:
www.newbusinessbreakthroughs.com.au

Or come and join in the conversation online at:-

www.facebook.com/peterlawson54

www.linkedin.com/in/peterlawson

Here's to your success...

Peter Lawson

CHAPTER 1

Starting Your Accounting Practice – No Capital Required

So you have just made the decision that you are going to start up your own Professional Knowledge Firm and you're wondering how it is all going to happen. Let's paint the picture here. You are currently working for a professional firm, still doing your tertiary education and you have no money. Believe it or not, this is a great starting point to commence the marketing of your own Professional Knowledge Firm.

THE STRATEGY

When you are a trainee in a professional firm the pay isn't that great. In fact, you are paying for your experience. You are paying to learn the tricks of the trade so to speak. So, if you are in a professional firm that is not progressive and does not provide on the job training, and you are not learning something new *every day*, then you need to move on.

You need to be working in the right environment for this strategy to work. And the right environment is one where you respect the quality of the work that the firm produces and can confidently refer clients to that firm because you know they will benefit from the experience.

This strategy is all about building your own client base and having the client base looked after for you until you are qualified and experienced enough to take that leap of faith and set up your own Professional Knowledge Firm. This is a win-win situation for both you and your employer. You will be marketing the firm you are working for (your employer), you will be providing warm to hot referrals, and your employer will be deriving fees from your client base. This client base comes at no cost to your employer and you will be appreciated by your employer for providing these referrals to the firm.

All that is required to make this work is that you have the following:-

- Some friends and acquaintances that are in business or know some people in business

- Good communication skills and an ability to gain rapport with people

- You are working for a firm that has a wide range of services to offer and is marketable

- Good back up from your employer

TIP: It is highly recommended that you start with a strategic plan so you can follow it in order to reach your goals. This is a great opportunity for you to build your own client base and have them serviced while you complete your qualifications and experience. This is like having your clients baby-sat while you are getting organised to start

THE STEP-BY-STEP PROCESS

You can get started on your client base while you are still employed. You must ensure that the firm you are working for is a progressive firm and that they can handle your client intake and provide the service that your client base will be seeking. You must also ensure that your employer provides additional services for their client base. Your employer should have some unique features that set them apart from other firms in the same market. You must have confidence in your firm and confidence in yourself.

The first thing you need to do is to prepare a list of all the people you know. Think of all the people on your list that could benefit by doing business with you and by using the quality services provided by your current employer. You don't have to list people that are necessarily in business or that have the potential to be a business client. We never make assumptions. People know people who know more people. Professional business is a people business and the strategy is to know lots of people.

Once you have made up this list you need to work on a script. That is, what you are going to say to these people when you inform them that you are working for a very ethical and forward thinking accounting practice that is looking for new clients who can benefit from their experience. At this point in time you should phone about ten people on your list and get a feel for their response. This will also enable you to refine and perfect your script. You need to test your scripts and record the responses to make sure you are asking the right questions. Measurement is important.

Now that you have made some calls and have an idea of how to approach your data base, you then need to sit down with your employer and put forward a proposal. I would assume that the senior partners in your firm are very busy. Let me tell you, they are never too busy when you want to discuss a proposal to bring more fees into the firm, especially at no cost or effort on their part.

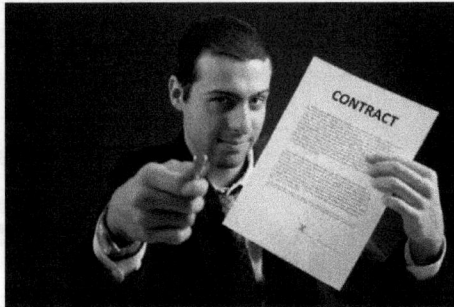

Before you have that all important meeting with the partners you need to put the proposal together. You need to know what's in it for them and also what's in it for you. If there is no what's in it for you, then they may be wondering why you are going to all this trouble. You must make sure that the client base is *your* client base and that the client base will move with you if and/or when you move on. This means there will be no arguments should the time come for you to move on to another firm or to start-up your own business.

It's called *'the deal before the deal.'*

The "what's in it for you" could well be a small percentage of the fees derived. Bear in mind, that if you are deriving some fiduciary benefit from the referral you need to let the referee know all about this benefit. You must at all times be ethical, honest and up front with any transactions or dealings. I personally would not recommend that you derive a fee benefit from these clients as there are all sorts of ramifications that could come back to haunt you.

Once you have prepared your proposal it is then time to meet with the partners and explain that you have a number of people that you believe could very well benefit from the services that they provide and further that you would like to refer these people to the firm. And you would like to market the firm's services to your data base.

To summarise the process:-

- Make a list of everyone you know
- Prepare a script for approaching these people
- Determine a strategy for approach
- Put a proposal together to meet with the partners of your firm
- Determine the benefits for these prospective clients
- Have a plan in place for the strategy

TIP: Work hard on your client base. Ensure that your employer can provide all the services necessary to cater for your prospective clients. Look at joining clubs in your local area that could provide you with prospective clients.

How It Works

At this point in the discussions you need to do the deal before the deal with your employer. This means that you must discuss the rules of engagement and this will be included in your strategy for discussions. And the rules of engagement are that you will be working with your client base on all aspects of their business, including taxation, business services corporate re-structure, even though these might be outside your scope of experience within the firm.

Let me explain the advantage of this...

Let's say you are working in the audit division of the firm, and the only function you perform is auditing. This means that you don't have much exposure to tax and business services. Now, provided you have done the deal before the deal and agreed on the rules of engagement, you will be working on every aspect of your clients' affairs, which means that you will now be trained in other services that are offered by your firm. And that is why it is important that the firm you work for covers a wide and diverse range of services. Another win-win situation for both parties. This means that your clients' needs and wants can be catered for by the firm. It also means that you can gain experience in a wide range of service offerings.

It all depends on the client's requirements; the more diversified the client's activities, the more potential for diversification of services that you can now be exposed to and gain experience with.

You are now gaining experience in areas other than audit and you are gaining that experience while you are working with your client base. And you are gaining the necessary experience that you will need to start up and grow your own Professional Knowledge Firm.

This is a win-win arrangement for all parties. Your employer is gathering new clients without any marketing expenditure. They do not have to spend as much time gaining rapport with the client before the engagement begins as you have done most of that for them. In addition to that, your employer is gathering new clients through the opportunity that you have created. They may never have had the opportunity to take these clients on board without your assistance. Your employer is deriving new fees. In addition to that, you are being trained in other service areas of the practice, which will make your employment far more interesting, and you are working with people you know. The firm will benefit from your training as you will have a more diverse range of expertise, which means they can charge more fees, which means you are more valuable.

You will not be bogged down in just one division of the firm, doing the same stuff day in and day out. You will learn something new every day of your working life and you will gain that much needed experience to start up your own accounting practice when the opportunity arises. This is the easiest way to gain experience and training in every aspect of your profession, and in addition to that you are being paid a wage while you learn.

To summarise how it works:-

- Do the deal before the deal

- Ensure that you will be working with all the clients that you have introduced to your employer

- Ensure that you will be gaining experience in other services that are provided by the firm

- Your firm must provide a wide range of services to suit your clients' requirements

  You will be trained in a variety of services offered by your firm

TIP: Always do the deal before the deal and draw up an agreement. It is always best to draw up agreements at the beginning while we are all friends. You must ensure that you will gain some benefit from the arrangement (apart from remuneration) in the form of training and experience.

WHY IT WORKS

Because you are showing enthusiasm by bringing in new clientele to your employer, the partners of the firm will appreciate this and will show this by spending more time with you. Their posture will change. Their attitude towards you will change and they will want to get to know you better. This means that you will be more exposed to the partners of the firm and by spending more time with them you will gain even more knowledge and experience, but this time, at the top level. They will have different discussions with you as they will be talking to you about your clients and their activities. You now have the opportunity to ask questions of the partners from the box seat.

In a professional firm if you are showing some incentive and enthusiasm, and going to the trouble of bringing in new work, then the whole game changes. You are really now becoming part of the team at the top; you are considered a rainmaker, a valuable asset to the firm. And when you are a valuable asset you are handled with care. This doesn't necessarily mean that you will be earning more money. That is not what the game is all about. The game is all about building your client base and building it without the stress and responsibilities that go along with maintaining a client base. Your employer is doing that for you. And in return you are allowing your employer to retain the fees. It is similar to a mother hen minding the little chicks as they grow.

You get to do all the good parts. You get to enjoy all the good aspects of dealing with the client and you don't have to worry about the administrative requirements that sit behind every client. Your employer does that for you. And remember, they are getting paid to do so.

Your clients are being serviced by your employer. You do not currently have the expertise or the time to do this without the involvement of your employer. You are involved in all the work and while you are involved you are gaining valuable on-the-job training and experience. This is gold. Your learning will be fast-tracked and your confidence will grow. The on-the-job learning will help you with your tertiary education as well. The theory that you have been covering at university will now start to make sense as it is applied at work and this will be explained in more detail with your on-the-job training. Your theoretical questions will be answered. You just don't get this kind of attention without that introduction of the client base to the firm.

When you are prospecting for new clients for your employer you are gaining valuable marketing experience. In some cases the prospective client may be substantial enough to warrant the attention of a partner of the firm at the initial interview. And, of course, you will also be attending that interview as well. You will get to see first-hand how the partner presents to the client and the technique they use to demonstrate the benefits of dealing with your firm. I am assuming of course that the partner attending these initial meetings is the partner responsible for bringing new clients into the firm and therefore experienced at converting the meeting into a new client. You will soon learn that the success of your practice is based on growth, and growth is all about taking on new clients of the type that you want. This means, not just new clients, good clients. When I say good clients, I mean clients that fit into your definition of 'ideal client.' The concept of determining your ideal client will be discussed in chapters three and four.

To Summarise Why it Works:

- You will gain valuable experience in all aspects of your profession

- You will be trained by the best in the business - the partners

- You will gain valuable marketing experience - essential for your own business

TIP: There is excitement in growing your practice. You must always grow a practice with clients 'of the type that you want'...yes the type of client that YOU want to deal with. You must create a definition of your ideal client and stick to it like glue.

THE BENEFITS

Introducing clients to your employer is a win-win situation. At this stage of your career you do not have the knowledge or experience to service clients. In addition to that, you really do not have the time to properly service the clients. You have a full time job and you are in the process of completing your tertiary education, and the tertiary education takes up most of your spare time outside of work.

This is a great time to start marketing for your own Professional Knowledge Firm - yes, your own practice. Even though you are out there looking for clients for your employer, you must think of it this way: your employer is actually baby-sitting the clients until you are experienced enough to look after them yourself. And while your employer is looking after the client you are gaining experience as you are involved with servicing the clients. And remember, the employer is deriving additional fees from your efforts...and for free.

When you join a Professional Knowledge Firm you are generally planted in one division of the firm and you tend to stay in that division until you make some noise. For example, you may start your employment with an accounting firm in the audit division. You generally tend to remain in the audit division for some time. Even though you gain valuable experience in this division, you are not exposed to taxation and other business services. This knowledge is essential if you are to start and grow your own Professional Knowledge Firm.

The whole game changes when you introduce clients to your employer. The partners take an interest in you because you are thinking of the best interests of the firm. This means you get to hang out with the partners more often. And the deal is that if you bring clients into the firm, you will be involved with servicing these clients, which means that you will be learning how to gain knowledge from all divisions within the firm. In some cases you will be dealing directly with a partner of the firm. And that is where you want to be. The partner is your greatest source of knowledge. The partner can also teach you how to become a partner. You will gain years of knowledge by just hanging around with the 'in' crowd.

In addition to learning a variety of skills, you will also learn how to market for your own business. When you introduce a substantial client to the firm, this will gain the attention of the partners. You must insist that you attend all meetings with your clients. And it is particularly important that you attend that initial meeting between the partner and the prospective client. This is where you will see the partner do his or her best work in presenting the proposal to the client. You will see first-hand how to conduct a meeting and how to win the client. This knowledge and experience is essential for growing your own business. In addition to providing great service you must know how to show what the benefits are of dealing with you and your firm. A good rainmaking partner will have these skills. This is not the type of skill you will learn at university. They do not show you how to build a business; they only show you how to do the business. There is no education on client conversion in economics, accounting or law courses, nor is there any in architecture or other professional courses. You would only gain this knowledge if you do a course specific to this activity. And have you got time for that?

Let's not forget the benefits to your employer. The firm will benefit from the additional revenue that will be derived from your client base. They have not had to spend time and money prospecting for these clients and they will spend little time in converting these prospects into clients because you have done all the spade work and provided a very warm lead-in. This is money for jam for the firm. The most important thing (and the most time consuming element) about selling is gaining rapport from the prospective client. You have already created this rapport with the prospective client. You have already informed them of all the services the firm has to offer. The conversion process is easy from there. All the partner has to do is to emphasise the benefits of dealing with the firm. There is no selling. All you have to do is give the prospective client a good reason to buy from you.

When you introduce clients to your employer on a consistent basis you get onto the partners' radar. You get to hang out with the partners as you are now considered a rainmaker and part of the team. By associating with the partners you gain knowledge and experience in just a few hours; knowledge and experience that would take years to obtain had you been just an ordinary employee that fronted up each day and did the same thing day in and day out, in the same division for years and, very likely, always overlooked for promotion. By working at marketing your employer you will build up a substantial client base. You will be promoted on a more regular basis as you gain more knowledge and expertise. You become a valuable asset to the firm and there may come a time when you are offered a partnership, at which point you have some nice alternatives; you can stay in your comfort zone within the firm as a partner or have a go out on your own and not die guessing what it would be like having your own very successful Professional Knowledge Firm.

There are no hard and fast rules about when to start your own business, this is a decision made on gut feeling. And you will get that gut feeling from your client base. At this stage you will have finished your tertiary education and have all the qualifications, experience and knowledge necessary to start your own Professional Knowledge Firm. You have a client base, which means you have income and cash flow. You don't have to spend a great deal of time and money developing your client base as you already have one. You don't have to allocate capital to purchasing another accounting firm or a block of fees as you already have them. And the clients are not strangers. You have already been working with them.

You introduced these clients to the firm and there will be no hard feelings when you decide to take them with you. Remember, that was the deal before the deal. Your employer has derived fees from these clients and it did not cost them a penny to get those fees on board. Your employer, although disappointed that you are moving on, should be proud that you are having a go on your own. If they do not have this attitude then I have some bad news, you have been working for the wrong employer. If that be the case then the good news is that you will not be working for them anymore.

The day you start your new business you will hit the ground running. In chapter five we will have a look at the advantages of having fixed price agreements with your clients; another win-win situation for both parties. When you are starting out you can use the fixed price agreement format to your advantage. And again we will be demonstrating the importance of the deal before the deal.

Let me explain:-

Before engaging with your clients, you should meet with them and discuss the benefits in having a fixed price agreement with your new Professional Knowledge Firm (these benefits will be explained in detail in chapter five). When you have agreed on the value of the fixed price agreement for the following 12 months of service, you will then arrange for the client to pay their fees in monthly instalments at the commencement of each month. This is also a good time for you to ask the client to pay three or six months in advance for your services, a retainer deposit so to speak. If you start out with a small fee base of $100,000 in fees and you receive three months fees in advance, that means you can open your bank account with a $25,000 deposit you won't have to borrow from the bank or withdraw from your own capital to cover establishment costs and overheads.

Does that make sense to you? And does this answer the next question: Where am I going to get the money to cover my establishment costs and my overheads for the first three months?

To Summarise the Benefits:-

- Your employer will be deriving fees from your client base

- You can grow your client base while still being employed

- You will fast-track your experience and knowledge by working with your clients within the firm

- You will have a client base when you make that decision to start up your own Professional Knowledge Firm

- You can start your own Professional Knowledge Firm without having to borrow money or use your own capital

TIP: Your employer can baby-sit your clients while you gain the knowledge and experience required to commence your own practice. When you start your own practice you will hit the ground running.

CASE STUDIES

Once upon a time there was a very ambitious trainee accountant that decided very early in the peace that he was going to start his own practice and he would do this as soon as he had the knowledge and experience to do so. That trainee was me. Let me tell you a little story that will help you understand how this whole thing works so that you can apply it to your own start-up.

Way back in my early days as a trainee I was going to work during the day and attending university at night. I was a very keen sailor and met and became friends with a vast number of people all over Australia, some younger, but most older than me. These people came from all walks of life, some were tradespersons, professionals, executives of large organisations, business owners, and the list goes on. I was a little different to most accounting trainees. I had an outgoing personality and I was also confident, without being cocky. And this helps.

Meeting and associating with a diverse range of people on a sporting platform was probably the best education I had. You see, the professions are a people business and, even though you have to have knowledge and experience to perform your duties, it is street smarts and common sense that get you the clients you need to start and grow your Professional Knowledge Firm. All I had to do was to get these people to a meeting and the senior partner of the firm would do the rest.

I was working for a small firm of chartered accountants in Sydney. They were a small firm that had some large clients, with large fees to match. They also had a few public companies that they audited. The main source of revenue for this firm was auditing and I was on the audit team. Now you may be saying, ' how boring,' but I have to say you learn a lot about accounting when you do audits. You also come across a diversified range of systems and processes. I had been working in the audit division for two years when I decided that I wanted to one day have my own accounting firm. I approached one of the partners of the firm and requested a transfer to the tax and accounting division. If you want to run your own show you must have diversification of skills such as tax, accounting and corporate.

Unfortunately, at the time, there was no full time position in the tax and accounting division so I was stuck with auditing for the time being. I didn't want to leave the firm as they were a great bunch of people to work for; less stuffy than most accounting firms.

It was then that I decided that I needed to know more about the services that the firm offered. And I needed to know more about the partners. There was one partner that was the main rainmaker for the firm. He did all the entertaining and was involved as a director on a number of company boards. I found out that this particular partner was a keen sailor. And I also found out that this particular partner knew some people I knew. So, one day, I tapped on his door and introduced myself and dropped a few names. His whole face relaxed as he invited me into his office. That day we chatted for over an hour about sailing, and the people we both knew in sailing. And this is where I gained my rapport with this very senior partner, the Big Kahoona.

An opportunity came up for me to work in the tax and accounting division of the firm. After three months I had gained enough knowledge to be confident about talking to my many contacts about coming on board as a client with my employer. I had a meeting with the partners of the firm to discuss my intentions of doing some marketing for the firm, in my own time, with the purpose of introducing some new clients to the firm. They were delighted and my senior partner (now new best friend), the chief rainmaker, opened the bar in his office and offered me a drink (don't be alarmed, it was at the end of the working day, not the beginning).

In less than two months I had introduced five clients to the firm. They were all small business owners. The (rainmaker) partner attended all the initial interviews with these clients, as did I. This partner was a magician at converting clients and I learnt so much, not only about this process, but about presentation and posture. He had a better than 85 percent strike rate, but bear in mind, the client was not a cold call but a very warm introduction from me.

There were some clients that I introduced to the firm that did not require an initial meeting with the partner. Nonetheless, I still had the opportunity to work on these clients under the supervision of a person more experienced than myself, which meant that I was still learning something new every day.

The prospecting continued and I introduced, on average, one new client per month. This meant I got to hang out with the senior partner at least once per month and observe the master at work. There were a few occasions when the partner would take me to lunch to thank me for the introduction of a new client. I learnt more at those lunches than I ever did in all my years at university. I used to write notes on the back of napkins.

After six months my nest of clients was really starting to grow. It was so much fun at Christmas time as I was allowed to attend all the Christmas parties for these clients and at all times, my partner friend would attend also as he also enjoyed a few drinks. So here I was, building my own client base, having the client base serviced by my employer, hanging out with the senior partner, building my knowledge and experience at a rapid rate, and most of all, having a great time.

After four great years with this firm, I made the agonising decision to move on. I had to make the move in order to increase my knowledge and experience in taxation and accounting and also to improve my skills in dealing with small businesses, as this was where I would have to start with my own Professional Knowledge Firm. I decided that

I had to work for a small practice in order to gain experience in all aspects of accounting, because in the smaller practices you have to take a client from start to finish and this is what I needed to learn; the whole process.

Before I started my job interview process, I did the right thing by my employer and sat down with the partners of the firm and explained that it was time for me to move on. Although they were not very keen on the idea, they completely understood as they knew that my ambition was to start my own firm one day. There was a suggestion that there could be an opening for me as a partner of the firm somewhere down the track, but I had it in my heart to start up my own practice, and to do so I had to broaden my knowledge and experience with a smaller firm. These are the painful decisions you have to make if you want to achieve what you desire. These are not easy decisions to make, especially when you have developed friendships and relationships in a firm and it is very hard to say goodbye.

I then commenced my interview process for a new employer. I was targeting smaller suburban accounting firms. At this point of time I had a client base valued at more than $20,000, and this client base was very attractive to all my prospective employers as these fees more than covered my proposed salary. I mentioned previously that the pay as a trainee was pretty ordinary, but bear in mind, this was 1978.

I had experience across all aspects of accounting and I was in my last year of university, with my professional year to complete as well. I needed to work for a firm that was small enough so that I would be handling every aspect of the client's work from start to finish, and I needed a firm big enough to support me through the rigours of the professional year that was in front of me.

I also had to do the deal before the deal in relation to my client base. The deal before the deal is that the client base will follow me if at any stage I move on, either to another firm or to set up my own practice. It was important with this agreement that I pointed out that the employer did not have to pay any remuneration for these clients to come on board, they would derive all fees from this client base during the period of my employment, and the client base would remain my client base and, accordingly, being my asset, I would be entitled to take this client base with me should I transfer to another employer or establish my own Professional Knowledge Firm. In other words, whatever I bring in, I take with me. And while this client base is being serviced by you, the employer, you will be entitled to all the fees from this client base.

The last thing you need is a dispute when you decide to start up your own Professional Knowledge Firm, so always do the deal before the deal. It is always best to draw up these agreements while we are all friends.

I finally settled on a five partner suburban firm that seemed to be quite friendly and was very open to the prospect of me marketing the firm for the purpose of introducing new clients. Who wouldn't be? Another aspect that encouraged me to choose this firm is that they were the largest firm in the area and were very well respected.

In this firm I worked very closely with one of the partners and we became quite good friends, especially as I introduced, on average, one new client per month to the firm. I did enjoy working at this firm, but all I was thinking about at this stage was getting the knowledge and experience I needed to start my own Professional Knowledge Firm, and when the time was right, and I had the necessary qualifications, I would make the quantum leap to start up my own firm.

TIP: Professional trainees are traditionally underpaid, compared to trainees in other industries. Professional trainees are effectively paying for their experience through reduced remuneration. So the day you stop learning as a trainee is the day you need to move on.

ACTION STEPS TO ASSIST WITH THE IMPLEMENTATION OF THESE STRATEGIES

In order to commence your own start-up, you must have a plan. And your plan must be to gain as much knowledge and experience as you can, however you can. The first thing you need to do is ensure that you are working for a pro-active accounting practice that you can be proud of, a firm that you are happy to market, and a firm that will look after your client base while you're in the process of building your business. There are six important steps to starting your own Professional Knowledge Firm:

- Work for a respected firm where you can obtain knowledge and experience, and most of all professional ethics.

- Ensure that your employer is a pro-active firm of accountants.

- Put a business plan together setting out what needs to be done to start up your own Professional Knowledge Firm.

- Create a list of prospective clients that you can introduce to your employer.

- Meet with your employer to inform them of your intentions with the introduction of new clients and seek their approval.

- Work on your marketing plan to ensure that you will have enough client base for the start up of your own Professional Knowledge Firm.

- The day you stop learning something with your employer is the day you need to move on.

CHAPTER 2

Getting The Show On The Road

The time has come for you to take the leap of faith to start up your own Professional Knowledge Firm. At this stage you should have enough fees in your client base to make that all important decision to move on and to venture out into the big wide world of business. If not, there are other alternatives and they will be mentioned in the latter part of this chapter.

THE STRATEGY

ASSUMING YOU HAVE A CLIENT BASE

Now that you have made that all important decision to start up your own accounting practice, you need to ensure that you do not burn any bridges and that you proceed with the start-up on a professional and ethical basis. The main aim here is to part friends with your employer. This means you need to sit down with the partners of the firm and explain that you have really enjoyed working with them, and that you have this yearning ambition to have a go out on your own. They should completely understand this, as they too once had that same yearning ambition. And bear in mind one or two of those partners would have done the same thing themselves when they started their own firm. The other thing is that they may offer you a partnership, which is an alternative for you to consider.

At this stage you should have a very good relationship with your client base and accordingly, be confident that they will follow you. The first thing you need to do is to have *that* meeting with your employer. Prior to that meeting, you need to put some points together to explain to the partners why you are moving on. It's important to let them know you are not moving on because you are unhappy with the firm, it's just that you want to have a go on your own.

At that meeting you need to have your agreement handy (*refer to the case study at the end of this chapter to demonstrate why this is important*) and give your employer some comfort in making them fully aware that you will only be approaching your own client base to discuss this move, and, at the same time, you will offer these clients the choice of remaining with the firm or moving on with you. It is important that you have this understanding with your employer as it is very likely that you will be starting your own Professional Knowledge Firm in a location close to your existing employer and what you really need from them is their support.

Meeting with the partners is the toughest part of this assignment. What you need to do next is finalise the strategic plan for your new business. Before you approach your client base, you will need to prepare a menu of services and also a proposal in relation to their fees. In order to differentiate yourself from other accountants, you should be approaching your clients with a fixed fee proposal based on your menu of services. Work on bundling these services for your client to demonstrate that they will be getting value. Provide the clients with all the information they need to make an informed decision about coming on board with you.

First things first, you will need to define your *ideal client*, i.e. those clients that meet your requirements. There may be some clients in your client base that do not fit this definition and accordingly there is no point approaching them to come on board.

Some examples of an ideal client would be:-

- A pleasant nature.
- Pay their fees on time.
- Act upon your advice.
- Can afford to pay your fees.
- Demonstrate potential for growth.
- A good advocate and referrer.
- Open to new ideas.

Once you have gained the support and approval from your employer, it is then time to approach your client base. You will need to meet with each of them individually to explain the situation, reassure them that your employer is aware of this situation and that they have the option of remaining with your employer or moving on with you. That is the ethical thing to do.

The next step is to have a meeting with each of your existing clients to confirm which clients are coming on board.

STARTING THE BUSINESS - WITHOUT YOUR OWN CLIENT BASE

In the first part of this chapter we looked at the scenario where you introduced clients to your existing employer and had an agreement with your employer.

There may be a situation where you are working for an employer and a number of clients have indicated that they would follow you if you were to commence your own Professional Knowledge Firm. Should this be the case, you must act ethically and approach your employer and inform them of this situation.

The best approach in this situation is to prepare a proposal for your employer which includes an offer to pay a fee for these clients that have indicated that they wish to join your new Professional Knowledge Firm. Arrange a meeting with your employer and explain the situation and come to an agreement. I would strongly recommend that you have your solicitor draw up an agreement detailing the acquisition of these clients from your employer. The next step is to meet with these clients to introduce your menu of services and also discuss the way you will be doing business in your new Professional Knowledge Firm, especially in relation to fixed price agreements and the bundling of services. You need to confirm that these clients are comfortable with the way you will be doing business in your new practice.

Always consider the importance of leaving your employment on good terms and that means behaving ethically at all times. These sticky situations do arise. Always be up front and deal with it so that nobody dies.

DO I PURCHASE FEES?

When commencing your own Professional Knowledge Firm you could also consider the acquisition of another Professional Knowledge Firm or the acquisition of a block of fees. Either way, there are some dangers here for young players.

The acquisition of fees will be dealt with in more detail in chapter four. There are plenty of other options available to you before you need to consider the acquisition of fees.

GETTING STARTED

The big day has arrived. You have made the decision to commence your own practice. Now the hard work begins. Your job role has now changed from technician to prospector and in the early days you will have to juggle both roles. That is why you need to start with a model of efficiency from day one. You need to consider outsourcing all of your compliance and administration work. You must also prepare systems and processes for checking that your outsourced compliance work is accurate.

Don't fall into the trap of doing the compliance work in order to save money. Compliance can be done more productively on an outsourced basis. It is your job to run the project and ensure the accuracy of the work done. Your role is to gather raw data from your clients, get this raw data to the outsourced compliance service, receive the finished product, review it for accuracy and then use the information to work with your client on the growth and profitability of their business. Compliance work does not improve the growth and profitability of your client's business, whereas measuring and managing will; this is what they want.

Too many professionals bore their clients to death by telling them how they arrived at the figures. The client doesn't want to know about the process, they only want to discuss the results and what the results mean.

I have conducted numerous Client Engagement Reviews for Professional Firms, and when we pose the question about outsourcing compliance work, the clients all agree that they have no concern who does this work, as long as it is reviewed by a competent person to ensure the accuracy of the completed job.

There are a number of companies offering compliance services. You must take the time to interview these companies to ensure that the quality of their work is at an acceptable standard. You must also ensure that the outsource company you deal with has all the necessary qualifications to prepare compliance work for you. One other thing you should also ensure is that the compliance company is accepted by your insurance company. It is important to ensure that your insurance company will cover any professional indemnity claims even though you are outsourcing your compliance work.

There are plenty of traps for young players. Just make sure you do your due diligence on any outsourcing entity before you engage their services. In considering the outsourcing of your compliance work, I would suggest you contact your Professional Association.

You should be outsourcing compliance work from day one, even if you are not very busy to begin with. Outsourcing of compliance work will free up valuable time for you to spend more effective time with your clients on how they can improve their business. Outsourcing will also free up valuable time for prospecting for new clients. Outsourcing should be the way you do business.

Now that you have established your initial client base you will need to prepare a budget.

The budget will help you make decisions as to whether you work from home, have a serviced office or obtain office space. If you are considering office space you need to look for space that has already been fitted out and you need to negotiate a rent-free period, especially if the space has been untenanted for a great length of time, say 90 days or more. The rent free period will help you with the initial costs and overheads associated with the establishment of the business. When you are having that initial interview with your clients you should include some questions that will give you an indication of how they would feel about you working out of home or a serviced office as opposed to your own commercial premises.

Setting up your own premises has benefits but it is an expensive option. You should consider how you are going to run your business. If you are going to be visiting your clients at their premises for all your meetings, then you don't have to have an office. You could save money by working from home. But you must also consider the cost of travelling and the time taken to travel. If your clients are coming to your office for meetings then you will be saving on travel time and could be utilising this time to market the business. You should seriously consider conducting your meetings online via screen share. This resolves the issue of travelling to meet with your clients and will save you a ton of time and money.

Serviced offices could be a good option. You have administrative services at your fingertip and there are no hefty fit out costs associated with setting up your own office. You could also give some serious thought to subletting some office space within another established office. This means you walk straight into a functional office space with no establishment costs and this established office could be a good source of referral, such as a law firm or financial planner.

As mentioned previously the most efficient option is to conduct your meetings via a screen share program. This way your client meetings can be conducted from anywhere, which means you do not need an office at all. There is a range of software to support this way of doing business. The main thing to consider here is the clients. They need to be comfortable. You need to demonstrate the benefits to your clients of conducting meetings over the phone; they do not have to spend time travelling to your office and can have meetings in the comfort of their own office.

The next item for consideration is software packages, such as your operating software and your office administration software. There are a number of options here. If you are outsourcing all of your compliance work then you may not need all of the operating software required to handle compliance work. There are a number of cloud based software packages that you can look at and they do not require any up front expenditure, just a monthly rental.

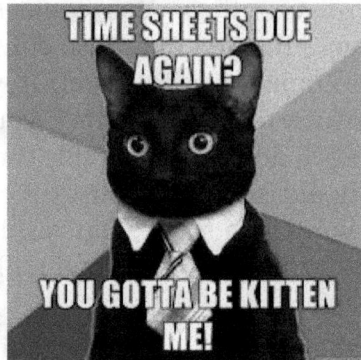

TIME SHEETS DUE AGAIN?

YOU GOTTA BE KITTEN ME!

I hope you are considering the option of fixed pricing with your clients.

Now that you have finalised your client base, you will need to prepare a strategic plan for the business and this will involve your vision and mission statements for the next three years (note: three years is a practical time frame for planning). You then need to look at where you want to be in three years and then chunk it down to two years and then one year, and even for the next six months. The plan will include an organisation chart setting out how the business will look when you have reached your three year vision. Initially, you will be covering all the positions on the organisation chart. In other words, you will be wearing all the hats, so to speak.

As you employ more people, or outsource more work, you will wear fewer hats as you will be delegating more and more. The goal is to be wearing just one hat at the end of the day. And that is your prospecting hat.

Initially, you should consider outsourcing all your compliance work and hiring virtual assistants to look after the administration. That will free up valuable time for meeting with your clients and discussing growth strategies.

To summarise your strategies:

- Ensure that you don't burn any bridges. Meet with your employer and be up front and honest about your intentions.

- Meet with the clients that have indicated that they want to come on board with you. Inform them of the way you will be doing business so that they can make an informed decision.

- Meet with prospective clients to demonstrate the benefits of coming on board with your new Professional Knowledge Firm.

- Prepare a strategic plan and a budget.

- Determine which software will be best suited to your success.

- Weigh up the options for premises based on client feedback.

- Outsource compliance work and administration work.

TIP: Planning is all important. Ensure that you make the transformation in an honest and ethical manner. Always remember not to burn bridges. You may want to cross them someday.

THE STEP-BY-STEP PROCESS

By the time you have made the decision to establish your own Professional Knowledge Firm, you will have a very strong indication from your client base that they are prepared to endorse this move. The most important thing is that you prepare a plan for the transformation process. The plan should include such things as: –

- Preparation for meeting with your employer to inform them of your intentions.

- Preparing for the worst case scenario should the need arise. This is your plan B.

- Preparation for the meetings with your client base to verify their endorsement.

- Preparation of a budget for the first 12 months, including rental for commercial premises.

- Preparation of a strategic plan for the next 12 months, and possibly the next three years.

Once you have your plan in place the next thing to do is to implement the plan. The first step in the process is to meet with your existing employer and explain why you want to establish your own practice.

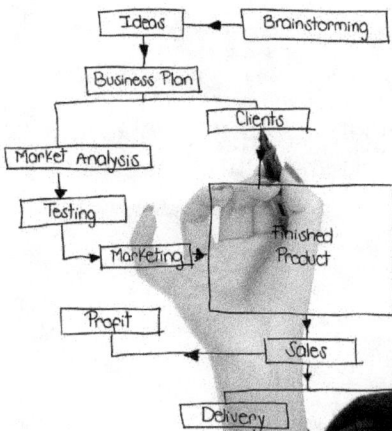

Now that the announcement has been made, you need to get down to the business end of the transition. It is now time to have that all important discussion with your employer about the client base that you have introduced to the firm, and that you will be approaching that client base to give them the option of joining you in your new business. You need to point out that this was the agreement from day one and that you would like to complete this process with as little disruption as possible.

You must always endeavour to leave your employer on a friendly and professional basis. You cannot afford to burn bridges. At this point of time, you need to agree with the partners on the date that you will be terminating your employment and also reassure them that you will leave the firm with a clean slate and that your work will either be completed or passed on to another team member.

The next step in the process is to prepare for those all important meetings with your client base. The most important thing is that you explain to your clients that the service level will not change. And it is important that you give the client an option to stay where they are or to take the journey with you. You should by now have a very strong relationship with the client and I would be very surprised if they would not be supportive of your move to establish your own business. There will be some instances where there are clients of the employer (that you did not introduce to the firm) that indicate that they would prefer to move on with you. This is a delicate situation and you must approach your employer and offer to pay an agreed remuneration for these clients. Just be up front and face the music.

With those meetings with the clients, it is a great opportunity for you to gather some feedback regarding office premises, what their expectations are regarding your new business, and any suggestions that they may have in relation to any additional services that they want.

This is also a great opportunity for you to present your new menu of services and to discuss with the clients the benefits for them in knowing the price for you services before the work is commenced. Again, we are doing the deal before the deal here and informing the client of the benefits of coming on board with you.

You should not throw too much at your clients in this initial interview. Just let them know that you will be commencing your own business by a set date. Inform them of the services you will be offering so they can then make an informed decision on whether to stay put or to follow you to your new Professional Knowledge Firm.

Before taking the option to go with your own premises, or even determining the size of the premises, you should consider the option of conducting all of your meetings by screen share. These are better alternatives than travelling, although I strongly recommend that you visit your clients at their premises throughout the year. They are house proud of their business and like you to visit them and show an interest.

If you decide to work from commercial premises you will need to determine the location for your premises; it would be prudent to leave some geographical distance from the location of your existing employer. You should look to obtain premises that have already been fitted out, in which case, your establishment cost will be low. You could also look at renting the furniture and equipment for the office in order to reduce your upfront costs. The location for professional offices is not that important. All you need to ensure is that the building is modern, clean and that there is plenty of parking available for your clients. Believe me, parking can sometimes be a very important factor. Convenience for your clients is of utmost importance, especially if you want them to have meetings at your office.

You should also consider sub-letting premises from a potential referrer. For example, if you were setting up an accounting practice there would be some benefits in subletting premises from an established legal practice where the fit out has already been completed for you and you will have your phone answered. You also have the opportunity of tapping into that client base. You will have meeting facilities and other benefits. It's food for thought. Other examples of workable sub-let arrangements could be with a financial planner, or any other business that deals with your target market but not necessarily in competition with you.

If you decide to work from home, you should also be prepared to travel to your clients' premises. In this case you must weigh up the cost of time spent travelling to your client premises. When you take this into consideration, it may well be more feasible for you to have commercial premises, in which case your clients would be coming to your premises for meetings.

It is then important that there is a plenty of parking available for the convenience of your clients. If you don't have appropriate parking facilities, your clients will always be running late for appointments, and so will you. In some Client Engagement Reviews, the clients have made some negative comments about the inconvenience of insufficient parking available for them when they visit their professional advisers.

Always look to negotiate a rent-free period with any commercial premises. This will reduce costs while you are establishing cash flow.

To summarise the Step-By-Step process:

- Prepare a strategic plan for the transformation process.

- Put a proposal together for your client base that will address their needs and wants so that they can make an informed decision to follow you onto your new practice.

- Meet with your client base to confirm the clients that will be coming on board with you.

- Determine whether you are going to work from home or from commercial premises.

HOW IT WORKS

When you are going through the transformation process, there will be some obstacles that pop up from time to time. Potentially the biggest obstacle you could face during the transformation process is the rejection of the proposal by your employer. As long as you have documented your agreement with the employer, that is, the agreement prior to joining the firm, then there should be no problem. This potential obstacle highlights the importance of doing the deal before the deal with the partners and this agreement should be drawn up by a legal practitioner to doubly ensure that this agreement can be enforced.

Having that meeting with the employer to discuss your transformation will ensure that there is no ill feeling and that you have their support. You can then agree on the date of the transformation process so that all parties, and in particular the clients, are not inconvenienced by the process.

You will have prepared a plan for this process. And now it is time to follow this plan. By meeting with the employer to explain your proposal you have overcome and avoided the main obstacle. Once you have completed this meeting, and all parties are happy, you can then go through the process of meeting with your client base to inform them of your intentions and to seek their approval. At that meeting with the clients, you will be able to inform them of the date for the changeover. By offering the clients the option of remaining with the firm you are behaving in an ethical manner and this will certainly be respected by your employer. You will also gain the respect of your client base in doing the right thing. You are also respecting their privilege of choice.

The meeting with the clients will be your opportunity to inform them of the way you will be running your business and also a great opportunity to introduce your menu of services and gain their feedback and approval. With some clients you may choose to discuss their fixed-price agreement for the ensuing year and possibly negotiate some payment upfront. Each meeting with the clients will be individually tailored to their personalities, needs and wants.

With all this preparation, you will start on the ground running the day you open the doors to your new business.

Included in the plans and the budget for the commencement of the new business, you should include an opening party where you will invite all of those clients that have agreed to come on board. You should also include spheres of influence in the local area, such as local business people, members of the local Chamber of Commerce, your local Member of Parliament and any other influential people. There may also be some target clients that you would like to invite to the opening party to mingle with your existing client base. This strategy works very well. You will be seen to be giving; always a great start to any relationship.

To summarise how it works:

- Prepare the plan for transformation.
- Implement the plan for transformation.
- Prepare for possible obstacles in the way.
- Open up your new office with a bang.

TIP: The all-important part of making a smooth transformation is to gain acceptance from your employer and then your clients. Always conduct yourself in a dignified and ethical manner.

WHY IT WORKS

When you prepare a strategic plan for the transformation process, all you have to do is follow that plan in order to successfully implement the process. It is important that the first person to know about your intention to commence your own practice is your employer. There is nothing worse than a partner of your employer firm finding out from some other source that you are intending to establish your own practice. This is not a great way to start negotiations. The partners of your firm have the right to be the first informed of your intentions.

When you have that meeting with your employer, to inform them of your intention to commence your own practice, there will be some disappointment for the partners. They are not only losing a valuable employee, they are a losing some client base as well. And this does not always go down well with all partners. That is why it is important for you to remind them that they too were once in your position, being ambitious and wanting to have a go on their own.

In the meeting you should also mention how much you have enjoyed working for the firm and that it was a very hard decision to decide to move on. Also mention that you would like to think that their door is still open to you to come in and have a casual chat and a cup of coffee from time to time.

There can be huge ramifications for not ensuring that you part company on a very friendly basis. There is a possibility that your employer may attempt to sabotage your new venture, and they can do this in a number of ways. So in order to prevent this from happening, you need to plan for this all-important meeting with the partners to ensure that the transformation process runs as smoothly as possible.

You need to emphasise to your employer that you will be giving each of your clients the option to stay with the firm or to follow you into your new venture. This will give the partners some comfort knowing there is a possibility that some of your clients may choose to remain with them. There may be some clients of the employer that indicate that they want to transfer their business to you. This should also be discussed with the employer up front and a remuneration for these clients agreed upon.

The gate is now open. You can approach your existing clients and any prospective clients outside your current employer. And this is a great opportunity to let the clients know how you will be doing business.

Ensure that you show the clients your entire range of service offerings. Never assume that they would not be interested in certain services. For example, do not assume that your client would not be interested in something like web design or marketing, or even re-financing their loans. You don't know until you ask.

This is also a great opportunity to determine the needs and wants of your client. You will need to emphasise the benefits for them in doing business with you. Don't discuss the process, just discuss the benefits. You need to have a different approach and you need to show that you will do things differently with the new business and that will always be for their benefit. You have the opportunity to show them how you differentiate from other accountants, i.e. you will agree up front on their fee for the next 12 months and they can pay their fees by convenient monthly instalments to fit in with their budget.

You can also emphasise the benefits for the client of outsourcing the compliance work. The benefit being that they will be spending more meaningful time with you to discuss what the information means instead of how it was prepared. That way you will only talk about the benefits to them and not the process.

Your menu of services should offer things they had never dreamed of. Look at offering services outside accounting, services that will make you a one-stop-shop for their convenience. You need to show the client that you can act as the project manager to assist them with the growth of their business. For example, you may offer marketing and IT services and web site design and monitoring for Search Engine Optimisation.

Most small business owners are technically good at what they do. And they will tell you that if you get them in front of a prospect they are a better-than-even chance of selling their product or service. The problem is that they have no idea about how to generate leads in order to get in front of that prospect. What if you could provide them with a marketing system that would help them generate all the leads their business can possibly handle. Now we are really talking about something different, something that other accounting firms may not be offering their clients. I mean... which accounting firm are clients going to be attracted to...the one with the $50K turnkey marketing campaign to start the relationship or the one that doesn't offer the $50k marketing campaign. Think about it.

Accounting clients would much prefer to deal with all this at one central point and would be happy for you to co-ordinate the process. After all, you are their trusted adviser.

So, here is your big opportunity to exhibit your new business and the way you will conduct it. It is also an opportunity to seek feedback and to gain approval. You could look at this as your first marketing exercise.

To summarise why it works:

- Being honest and upfront with the employer will eliminate any obstacles to the commencement of your new business.

- A great opportunity to create a dynamic menu of services and present it to your clients for feedback and approval.

- Offer your clients something out of left field, like a marketing program that will help them generate leads for their business.

- By giving the clients the option to stay with the existing practice you will ensure their support.

TIP: Ensure that your employer is the first to know of your intention to commence your own business. This is not only common courtesy it is the ethical thing to do.

THE BENEFITS

By setting out a plan of attack for the transition into your own business you are setting out a process to ensure that all bases are covered. The benefit of meeting with your employer first and foremost is that they won't hear about your move from somewhere else. This situation could be embarrassing for all parties concerned.

Parting ways with your employer on a friendly basis will ensure that you don't burn any bridges. Sure, they won't be too happy about losing you and a bunch of clients. By scripting your approach you will at least be able to soften the blow.

Gaining permission to approach your own client base allows you to plan for the establishment of your business. You have the benefit of gaining some feedback from the client base on their expectations from you. And you will know for sure how many clients will be coming on board. This is also a great opportunity to introduce your new menu of services and also an opportunity to commence your fixed price agreements with the clients that are joining you. This is also an opportunity for you to do the deal before the deal and explain the way you will be doing business in your new-look accounting practice. If they don't like the way you will be doing business this is the best time to find out. This is also a great opportunity to introduce some very different services (such as a marketing system) This is a great way to differentiate yourself from other accounting firms.

By doing the right thing by your employer and your clients you will be going into your new business without any hitches. By carrying out this process professionally and ethically you will be starting your own business with everyone's best wishes at heart. You will gain support from your clients and will know where you stand because you have been upfront and honest with everyone. By knowing exactly where you stand the budgeting process is made much easier.

To summarise the benefits:-

- Your plan will ensure that the whole process is transparent with all parties.

- Your honesty and integrity will ensure that you know where you stand with your employer and your clients.

- When you confirm your position the budgeting process is made easy.

- This is a great marketing opportunity to bring on clients outside your existing client base.

- Nobody died.

QUOTE: Honesty is not the best policy... It is the ONLY policy.

CASE STUDIES

Well, here we go with another real life case study. And this one comes from my own experience when I made that leap of faith and commenced my own accounting practice.

The day finally came when I decided that I had sufficient knowledge and experience to commence my own Professional Knowledge Firm. I've gotta say, I was not 100 percent happy working in the firm I mentioned earlier and so the decision to move on was not difficult. My client base had now grown to a sufficient level to support my overheads for the next six months. And now it was time to put together my plan of attack. At this stage I had been working very closely with my client base and I was very confident that once I approached them about my proposed new business they would all come on board. But before I could approach my clients and confirm this, I had to do the right thing and approach my employer to inform them of my intentions. You see the area where my employer was located was a very close-knit community and had I even whispered my intentions to anybody, there was a better than even money chance that it would spread like wildfire around the community and my employer would hear about it second hand; not a good look.

Then came the part where I had to inform the partners of my intentions. Fortunately I already had an agreement with the employer regarding my client base. The clients that I introduced to the employer prior to my employment were stated specifically on that agreement. However I was concerned about the new clients that I had bought in after I commenced my employment. These clients were not specifically stated on the agreement but my solicitor pointed out a clause in the agreement that covered this situation. The lesson to learn here is always engage competent professional advice. Cheap advice can be very expensive.

Needless to say, I still had to gain the confirmation from the employer about all the clients that I had introduced to the practice.

I prepared an agenda and script for the meeting. Becoming a partner of the firm was not an alternative. Apart from the fact that I did not really want to stay, there was no real opening for a new partner in the firm anyway; something I considered favourable.

Finally the fateful day arrived and I approached my direct partner and indicated that I would like to have a meeting with all the partners of the firm. The founder of the firm, and most senior partner, did not attend the meeting. That was not good as that meant they would have to make a decision without him and this was not likely because of his often dictatorial nature.

Sitting in a room with the four partners, I started to get nervous and sweat formed in the palm of my hands. Fortunately, I still had my plan and script. I handed out the agenda for the meeting which meant I had some control of the meeting. The partners started reading the agenda and I noticed a few were shaking their heads, especially with the item on the agenda that required their consent for me to approach my client base to discuss their options.

At that point one of the partners said they would have to think about the matter. Typical procrastinating prick I thought, but I asked him what there was to think about. He said they would have to think about their consent for me to approach my client base. Fortunately, I was armed with our initial agreement regarding this particular item. I read out that particular part of the agreement so it was clear to all parties on what we had all agreed on two years prior when I joined the firm.

The other three partners nodded, but he mentioned that the absent partner, the one that did not wish to attend the meeting, would need to be informed, after which a decision would be made. This partner was in the office at the time so I suggested they invite him to the meeting so that the matter could be resolved immediately. This time the senior partner decided to attend the meeting. I then went over the items on the agenda that had already been discussed and in particular the agreement that I could approach my own client base.

NOTE: There is a lesson here for young players. Always make sure all the decision makers are in the room before you commence your presentation. Don't open the door for procrastination. Accountants tend to excel in procrastination.

I had to force the issue here, so I threw down a line that I had been working on. And at this point of time I have to make a confession. There was one person that I had informed about my intentions to commence my own business, and that was my solicitor. I knew he could keep a secret and, besides all that, I needed to discuss my strategy with him.

So I looked the partners in the eye and said to them, 'All of you must have had some ambitions at some point in your career or you wouldn't be partners in this firm.' I then directed myself to the most senior partner, and said, 'When you commenced this business I'm sure you had to leave your employer, and I'm sure that there were some clients that followed you to your new business.'

I went on to say that I really had no alternative but to commence my own business as there was no room for a new partner in the firm and I didn't want to ever die guessing what it would be like to have my own business. Once I had got them to review their own actions and think about it, they had to agree with me. The end result was they gave me their best wishes...*Mission accomplished.*

The partners also confirmed our agreement and because they had shown some element of doubt previously, I suggested that this would be a good time to list all the clients that I had introduced to the firm and confirm that these were my clients in accordance with the agreement. I also sought written permission to approach these clients to inform them that I was commencing my own business.

In order to give the partners a degree of comfort, I also informed them that when I have those discussions with my client base I would give them the option to remain with the firm or to follow me. They agreed that this was more than fair. All I wanted to do was to ensure that my employer understood my intentions and that there were no hard feelings.

I won't bore you with any more attention to detail about that meeting. The point of the matter was that I had done the right thing and the employer was the first to know about my intentions, apart from my solicitor. Had I not drawn up that all-important agreement, the deal before the deal, there would have been some serious issues with me approaching my own client base that could have resulted in litigation somewhere down the track. This is a lesson to be learnt for all young players.

Well that was the hard part out of the way. The next item on the agenda was to prepare a plan for the approach to my client base. Again, I had to put a plan in place for this strategy and along with this plan I had to have appropriate scripts for each client. I also looked at these meetings with the clients as being an opportunity to introduce my new menu of services. The firm that I worked for did not have a menu of services, so I was already differentiating myself from other accounting firms. This meant I was demonstrating the benefits to the clients.

At this point of time, fixed-price agreements had not been invented. I picked up the idea of menu of services from a mate of mine at university. This turned out to be a real deal clincher with the clients.

Then came the meeting with each of the clients I had introduced to the practice. Before these meetings, I prepared a questionnaire for them in order to ascertain what their expectations would be from me in the new business.

Through this questionnaire, the clients gave me some great feedback and I was able to tailor a marketing plan from this information. I went into these meetings with carefully scripted proposals. I also kept my word and offered every client their option to remain with my employer. With my carefully scripted proposals, my questionnaire and my menu of services, I was able to convert 95 percent of the client base that I had introduced to my employer. So I guess they had a five percent win. I was not concerned about these clients remaining with them and actually it was advantageous to me as it was confirmation to the partners that I had given the clients the option to remain with my employer.

By the way I did not even consider poaching any clients.

At that meeting with the partners, where I disclosed my intentions, there was agreement made on my date of departure from the firm. I worked my butt off to make sure I completed all my tasks and that I left with a clean slate. Because of this I gained the respect of the partners and my peers. This was very important to me both personally and professionally. Remember; always let your conscience be your guide.

Now that I had my employer's consent I approached my client base and was able to ascertain who was on board and who was not on board. From this exercise I also had a very good idea of my minimum fee base for the next 12 months. This was great for budgeting purposes. I have always found that the hardest part of a budget is determining the revenue, the expenses are easy.

I officially started my own business on 1 May 1980. I had a two month build-up to the end of the financial year when the office would get busier. This would be a very quiet period for me, cash flow wise, so in order to generate some cash flow I contacted all of my clients and suggested that we conduct a review of their financials in order to determine their position in relation to income tax liability. Back in those days, with small business clients, it was accepted that you prepare their financials once per annum and also prepared their income tax return and other compliance items. This meant that most businesses were running blind for 12 months of the year and were really only guessing at their income and their taxation liability. This new service ended up being a win-win situation. I had to produce some revenue between May and the end of the financial year (30 June). This was revenue that I would not have derived without this new idea. The other side of the win-win scenario is that my clients were able to sleep better at night. You see, they now had a set of financial statements showing their income to 31 March. This meant that we could calculate, with reasonable accuracy, the income to the end of the financial year and estimate the income tax liability... *Better the devil you know than the devil you don't know.* In addition to all that, I only had to complete the compliance work for three months of the year instead of 12 and this reduced my time to complete the end of financial year requirements.

QUOTE: Knowing the worst news is better than guessing what the bad news might be... Peter Lawson

ACTION STEPS TO ASSIST WITH THE IMPLEMENTATION OF THESE STRATEGIES

The Action Plan to Move Forward in Starting Your Own Business:-

- Prepare a strategic plan for the transformation to your new business.

- Prepare a budget to ensure that you don't run out of money in the process of setting up your new business.

- Prepare agendas for any meetings required in the process.

- Prepare a script for your proposals.
- Always be armed with information.
- Determine your points of differentiation.
- Always work towards a win-win scenario.

TIP: Never fear failure. Failure is your investment in experience...I would much prefer to fail than to die guessing what could have been.

CHAPTER 3

Positioning Your Accounting Practice For Growth

When you ask a real estate agent what to look for when buying a property, the agent will always respond with those three words, 'position, position, position.'

When you ask a business coach about how to grow a business, the response will be very similar, 'positioning, positioning, positioning.'

Positioning is the most important task in building your business and it's got nothing to do with the location of your business. Positioning is all about posture.

Corporate Hierarchy Structure

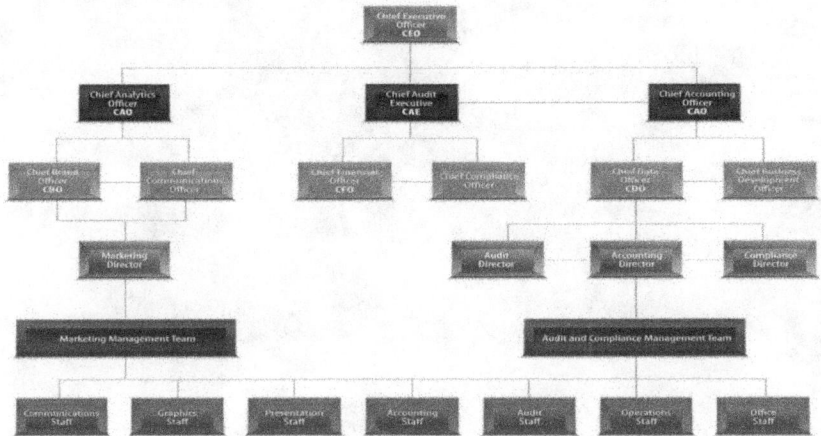

Let's now set the scene. You have taken the leap of faith and have finally convinced yourself to let go of the security of being employed and venture to the land of the unknown - owning your own business and all the fun that goes along with it.

It is at this point of time that you need to ask yourself the following questions: –

- Do I need an office, and if so, where do I locate?

- What are my clients' (and prospective clients') expectations from my business?
- Do I charge my clients on a time basis or do I offer fixed pricing?
- What are my software alternatives?
- What is the definition of my 'ideal client?'
- How do I position myself and my business?
- What work am I going to outsource?
- Who are my ideal team members?
- What operating systems do I use for office administration?
- Where do I start with my marketing plan?

THE STRATEGY

Positioning plays a major role in your marketing process. You must market YOURSELF and your business. Positioning yourself as an expert in your field is essential to growing your business. You can position yourself and your business in a number of ways:-

1. Web Site

This is a good place to start your positioning. You don't need to invest huge dollars to create an effective web site. The web site is the electronic doormat to your business. Everything you do out there in the way of promotion will be directed back to your web site so it has to capture the attention of your prospects. It has to have that WOW factor.

One thing I will bring to your attention here is that web site designers, although very good at creating beautiful looking web sites, are not marketing people. You need to seek advice from a marketing professional to ensure your web site will capture the attention of your prospects. You don't get too many chances here.

On your web site you need to cover four essential items. I call this my marketing equation.

Firstly, you need to find out the concerns of your prospective clients. You need to find out where their pain is and you need to interrupt that pain by entering the conversation going on inside their head. For example: Small business owners could be concerned that their accountant is too busy to talk to them and this is indicated by the fact he/she do not return their phone calls. Your web site would address this issue with a headline that said something like this...

> "Are you sick and tired of waiting for that essential call from your accountant so that you can make that all-important business decision?"
>
> And the sub-heading could be something like...
>
> "We understand and that's why we guarantee our clients that we will return all enquiries within five business hours."

Let me explain...

To be successful, your web site must firstly INTERRUPT. This means that the main heading on your web site must enter the conversation going inside your prospects' head. Once you have entered the conversation going on inside your prospects' head and you have interrupted them, the second thing you need to do is ENGAGE. This is the sub-heading. And by engagement I meant that you must offer some solution to the problem. Statistics show that you have only three to five seconds to capture the interest of your prospect to encourage them to read on. If not, they are gone, and possibly gone forever.

So, after you get the attention of your prospect, you must then EDUCATE them. You must provide them with some educational information to enable them to make an informed decision to buy from you. On your web site you should offer a report. Something like: …

"The Ten Things You Must Know Before Choosing An Accountant For Your Business."

In order to get this report the prospect must provide their name and email address in the box provided. And at that point you have their details so you can then provide them with some more information…called a drip campaign… to help them make that all important decision to purchase from you.

Did you know that only 3-4% of prospects visiting a web site are ready to buy now? So you need to give them something to remind them of you. And that something is that report and also the information that you will be sending them via email to allow them to make that informed decision to buy from you.

If other accounting firms are not offering education on their web site, who do you think the prospect is most likely to call when they are ready to buy, the accountant giving something away, or the accountant that doesn't?

Now that you have educated the prospect, the fourth part of the marketing equation is to OFFER them something to make them want to enquire further. This may be an opportunity to offer a risk free guarantee or the opportunity to offer a complimentary free "Second Opinion" meeting with you. Taking the risk out of the offer means that the prospect has nothing to lose. The main thing to remember with your marketing is that you become the obvious choice for your prospects to buy from you.

Your web site can also be used as your electronic store to sell product. Yes, that's right, the accounting firm of today needs to create product for sale via their web site. Think of some of the services that you provide that could be converted into a product. Again, when you are selling a branded product, you are getting your name out there. And that is what positioning is all about, getting your name out there. Today's marketing is all about people finding you, not you going out and finding the people. So the name of the game is to stick out like a sore thumb so that your target audience can find you and buy from you. And you will notice that I refer to your target market as an audience. They are your audience and you must think of yourself on stage at all times and think about this before you walk out the door. You have to ask yourself the question, "Am I looking my best?"

I also mention prospects buying from you as opposed to you selling to them. Selling went out the door some time ago. With all the information available today prospects are more savvy and you will insult their intelligence by trying to sell to them. And isn't that good news for all you accountants out there because we aren't trained to sell.

Completing your web site is only just the beginning. You see so many web sites out there that are tired and cumbersome. People are time poor and a slow web site will turn them off. Once you have your web site up and running it then becomes a work in progress that needs attention on a regular basis.

2. The Power of Video

Videos are a good way to get your message across. With Google now owning You Tube videos are something that can help you climb the Google rankings. Again, there is a right way and a wrong way to do videos and I have seen some shockers, especially with accounting firms.

This is one area where you must seek professional marketing advice to ensure prospects look at your videos and pay attention. And this is where the marketing equation is very important.

I will let you in on a little secret. The best videos all have great sound. I see so many businesses trying to do videos on the cheap. A cheap video will make you and your business look cheap. Positioning is all about you being the obvious choice when it is time for your prospects to buy and a cheap video won't help with that decision.

Videos can be used in a number of ways to position you and your business. Arrange for someone to interview you about the benefits of having you as their accountant. This video is an opportunity to show how your firm is different from other accounting firms. And what makes you the obvious choice when choosing an accountant. If you are wondering what to say here, go back to your marketing equation.

People are different in the way they absorb information. Some are visual. For this person the video would attract their attention. Some people are auditory and a recording would be more appealing. And some people would prefer to read something, so you provide them with some text. If you cover these three areas you are a better-than-even chance to attract prospects to your firm.

Also, consider having someone interview three of your clients about how much they benefit from being a client of your accounting firm. I have previously mentioned the menu of services. Make a video on your menu of services and make it interesting. Give people a reason to enquire. Then give your prospects a reason to want to buy from you. All you need is the opportunity to meet with a potential client, the rest is easy.

TIP: You could offer video interviews and testimonials as part of your service offering. How would your clients like to be interviewed and placed on your You Tube channel? What about a business of the month segment on your web site? Did we just find another product on offer from your business? Think outside the square here.

3. <u>Write a Book</u>

The word author is short for the word "authority." And you become an authority once you write a book. A book is a great positioning statement (I can personally vouch for that). A book will open doors for you. The fact that you have written a book can be a real deal sealer when prospecting for clients. And here you are saying you don't have time to write a book. What a load of rubbish. You can write a book in less than eight weeks, or you can engage the services of someone to write the book for you.

The game changes when you are running around town with a book under your arms. There will be a number of occasions when a potential client will mention that they have a particular problem with their business. How would you feel if you could hand them your book and say, 'have a look at chapter five in my book, it will help you with your issue.' Oh, and by the way, would you like me to sign it for you?

Do you think you have a better than even chance of converting that potential client? You bet you do.

What about this scenario. You're talking to a potential client who notices that you have a book in your hand and the book has your photo on it. Just watch the person's eyes move from you, then they look at the book cover, then back to you again as they verify that it is actually you on the front cover. And then they all of a sudden interrupt the conversation and say 'hey, is that you on the cover of that book?' There are no prizes for guessing the next topic for conversation. Can you see how that book can create some early rapport with you and that potential client?

The situation with a book is that your pre-eminence does tend to fade away in about 30 days. I mean, let's face it, where do you think the book is going to end up about one hour after you have left the meeting…that's right…on the bookshelf. And where do you think the book will stay? …you guessed it.

So to keep that pre-eminence going for longer than a month you have to come up with something that is going to remind the prospect that you are around. For that purpose I have my E-Learning System which is 52 chapters in a book, with 52 weeks of education in the form of video, audio and text. When the prospect is receiving education from you on a weekly basis how likely will it be that they will take your call in 60 or say 90 days? ...Pretty darn good.

4. Newsletters

The old newsletter has been around for a while. I would have to admit that I tend to bin the majority of newsletters, especially those from professional firms. The reason why? Let's face it *they are boring*. So, if you want people to read your newsletters they have to have some eye-catching stuff - something outside the square that's sexy.

If you want to know how to do this, refer to the marketing equation mentioned earlier in this chapter.

A newsletter is a very inexpensive way of telling people about your business. You can have a newsletter on your web site or you can email the newsletter out to your clients and to prospective clients. A newsletter builds your profile. It keeps you top of mind. Mailing out the newsletter can also have its advantages. Everybody receives emails these days and I recently learnt that people are opening only 14% of emails. They tend to just delete when they are busy. But receiving something in the physical mail box is something of a novelty. It's like opening a present. The recipient is intrigued.

Can you see the reason why you would send something in the post? Put simply there is a better chance of it reaching your target prospects. This concept could also be applied to important marketing material, especially to prospective clients. Even put it in a box with a big red bow.

You may even consider charging a subscription fee for your newsletter. When the newsletter has some value attached to it, people will appreciate it more and will be more inclined to read it. Make sure you include some interesting topics. And always remember to put some offers in your newsletter. Your clients may even want to advertise in the newsletter (I think we just found another product).

Put the boring technical stuff at the back of the newsletter. Things like information on taxation, accounting and legislative changes. These articles are a great cure for insomnia. An article about ten strategies to drive more customers to your business will certainly attract more attention.

The other advantage of putting a value on your newsletter is that it can be used as a bundling (or add-on) item when putting a proposal together for a prospective client.

5. Social Media

Before you go down this path you will need to read some books and attend some seminars so that you get it right. There is a fine line between exposure and what can be seen as obvious selling and abuse of the system. If you step out of line here you can find yourself barred from sights such as LinkedIn.

If you are a left brain thinking professional (like me), I would strongly recommend that you seek some assistance with this from someone who knows what they are doing. This is something that you can outsource very inexpensively.

Social media is also a very inexpensive form of marketing. There are so many alternatives available, such as LinkedIn, Facebook and Twitter just to mention a few. Most business owners make the mistake of just registering on these social media sites and do not put any time into their profile. Some do not even include a photo.

SOCIAL MEDIA

Content   **Networks**

{ status updates
blogs
videos
profile pages
websites

{ social media sites
video distribution
online communities

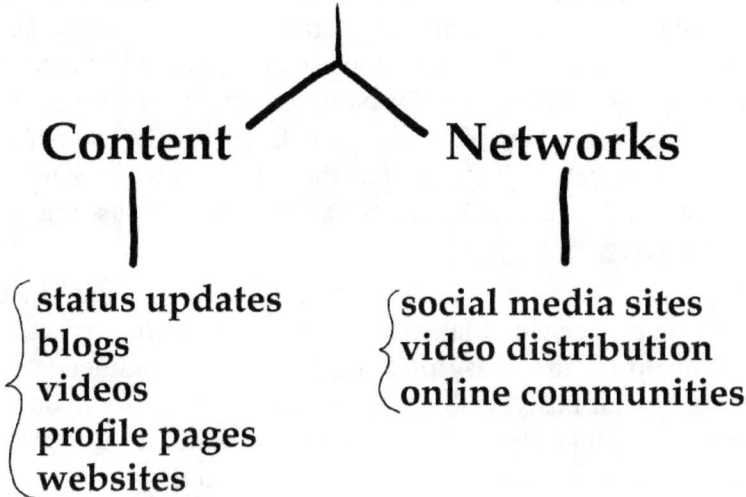

For the purpose of this exercise I will look at strategies for LinkedIn. And these can certainly be applied to other social media channels.

You may at some times be tempted to include a link to a landing page on your web site. Don't be tempted. If people want to know more about you they will have a look at your profile. And you can develop a process to engage with those people.

You must continually work on making adjustments to your profile in order to attract attention. I recommend you join groups relevant to your business that will benefit from doing business with you. You could also make contributions to these groups by commenting on questions that are raised within the groups. Also look for groups that are doing business with your prospects and are not in direct competition with you. There are benefits for both parties here.

You should determine the best days to visit these LinkedIn sites and mark down these days in your calendar. And you should make your comments at the same time on the same days each week. With this consistency there will be people constantly looking out for your comments and you will build a following. You see, you have to give something away first before you can start the selling process. And in a number of cases, accountants ask for the sale just one step too early.

There is a fine line between being helpful on social media and being seen as blatantly using social media as way to drum up business. By offering tips and recommendations on a regular basis, with no pitch an no expectation, you will have a regular stream of prospects looking at your profile and wanting to learn more about what you do.

6. <u>Live Presentations and Webinars</u>

If you have a fear of speaking, get over it. And if you can't get over it, attend some workshops that will assist you to do so. Public speaking and presentations are enormous strategies to lift your profile. You are seen as an authority and an expert in your field and potential clients will gravitate toward you. Presentations are a great way to get your message across to a large group of people in a very short space of time. Even a small group can be beneficial.

When you are presenting, you are holding court. Provided you are a reasonable presenter, people will want to learn more and that means they will want to meet with you to find out more. A good quality presentation with accurate and informative content will ensure a great conversion rate at the end of the session. Arranging a meeting is considered a conversion. Remember, on first meeting a potential client you are not selling products or services, you are selling a meeting. At that meeting you develop rapport with the prospective client. Also at that meeting you then sell an offer, a free offer that will benefit the prospective client. And the selling process goes on from here. I call this the 'Seven Drip Theory.'

Presentations are an essential part of positioning you and your business. You can choose to do these free of charge as a service to the local community. This is great way to position yourself as a good corporate citizen. This will help to lift your profile. On the other hand you could make a business out of presentations. Either way you will be exposing yourself to potential clients. There will always be potential clients in the audience. There is also potential for those attendees to tell people about your presentation. It is all about getting the word out there and letting people know you exist, and also letting people know how you can benefit them with the services that you offer.

And, let's not forget your existing clients, they too can benefit from these presentations. Internal presentations are also a great opportunity to introduce a new product or service to a number of clients at the same time. This will save you some shoe leather. And of course, following the presentation you throw on some bevies and have a chat with your clients about the new services. Remember, don't give too much away when you mingle as all you are trying to do is arrange a meeting.

With internal presentations, you should encourage your clients to bring along a couple of friends and colleagues. This gives your client an opportunity to show their friends and colleagues that they have an amazing pro-active accountant and they are in good hands. This also gives you a great opportunity to sell a meeting to these potential clients. Your client will help kick off the all-important rapport process.

Webinars, just like live presentations, are a great way to get the message across to a wide range of clients and prospective clients. There are a number of webinar packages out there that have different features. You should be looking for a webinar package with a good registration feature. This will certainly save you some time. You should also ensure that the webinar system contains a recording function. By recording your webinars you can run them time and time again without having to spend the time to present. You can also give these away as gifts to your clients and prospective clients.

The big advantage of webinars is that you can put them on at any time of the day. Participants can watch the webinar in the comfort of their own home and even in their pyjamas if they so desire. As a matter of fact, you can even do them in your pyjamas. Convenience is a big factor these days and the easier you make it for people to attend, the better the conversion rate.

You could also look at hosting your own 'ask the expert' call once per week or fortnight. This could be an open forum where clients and prospective clients can join the group, listen in, and even ask questions. You could put a value on the 'ask the expert' forum. When you give clients and prospective clients access they will perceive value in that access and there will be a much better chance of them attending.

 It costs the same to have 20 on the call as it does to have 100 on the call (depending of course on the software you choose for this exercise). And speaking of software, we use Go to Webinar. It has all the features you need for a successful meeting, is very easy to use and the monthly fee won't break the bank.

7. <u>Throw a Party</u>

Casting seminars and webinars aside, if it's bums on seats you want then you should consider throwing a party. To ensure a good return on your entertainment dollar you must ensure that you have a brilliant offer to announce at the party. Not a pitch and certainly not a hard sell, just an offer.

The offer could be something like free access to your weekly 'Ask the Expert' call.

Oh, and one very important thing about throwing a party... make sure you don't serve cheap booze; you don't want to get yourself a bad name for skimping on booze.

To ensure you get the best 'bang for your buck' you should give careful consideration to the invitees. Look at some spheres of influence and some prospective clients. Examples of spheres of influence could be your local politician, a prominent business person, entertainers or sports people.

Timing is everything here. If they've had too much to drink, they won't remember and if they haven't had enough to drink they won't listen.

Any announcements should be very short and crisp and have an impact on the audience. Consider making three very short announcements rather than just one big one. It is then up to you and your team to work the room and arrange some meetings.

Always determine what business you anticipate from the event and then work on the budget. Remember what you are selling here is not a product or the service, but a meeting. At the meeting you are better positioned to sell the product or service. The meeting also gives you another opportunity to develop and/or strengthen rapport with the client. And if you are thinking how much you should spend on the soiree you could start by calculating the lifetime value of your average client.

Rapport is the first item in the courting process. Without it you will find it very hard to move forward, but with it, you have the confidence of the client and they will buy from you, as opposed to you selling to them. There is a big difference between the two. Getting the client to first base is the hard part. Working on the conversion is easy. To give you an example... getting the first date with my wife was hard...getting to the proposal was easy.

8. Networking

In addition to the above strategies, there comes a time when you just need to get out amongst the people and stand belly to belly and have a good old-fashion chat. There are a number of things you need to learn about how you conduct yourself out in the public with meeting groups and networking events. Remember, at all times, in the process of developing rapport with people, you need to take the slow road. And the slow road means that people need to get to know you before they will do business with you. So you really need to get one thing straight here. When you first meet people never try to sell your services or products. All you need to do is to sell a meeting and that meeting is your first step into developing rapport. The old Seven Drip Theory.

The main thing to remember about positioning is that you have to stand out from the pack. You must show that you are different. At the end of the day, business is just a game and *differentiation* is the name of the game.

To be successful at networking events you must have an elevator pitch. And your next question is...'what is an elevator pitch?'

Well an elevator pitch is a clear, powerful and well-thought-out statement of your business's most compelling value that you can deliver anytime, anywhere, on the spot - in about 30 seconds. Your core message is your Unique Selling Proposition (USP)...

Your elevator pitch is your business' DNA written as a statement.

I have a special seven step process for successful networking and this will be exposed in the next section of this chapter under the Step-By-Step Process.

TIP: If you are a business person, and dealing with people, I strongly recommend you consider an NLP course

(Neuro Linguistic Programming). There are plenty of NLP courses around, some better than others.

THE STEP-BY-STEP PROCESS

Positioning yourself and your accounting firm is all about getting out there. You need to plan the positioning of your firm and to do so you need to identify every positioning strategy available. I have mentioned only a few positioning strategies. If you give this some serious thought, you should be able to come up with at least 30 items to better position your business.

You then need to prioritise these strategies and then you need to implement them. Regarding the implementation process, you will need to set a budget and you should consider outsourcing as much as you can. These strategies do take up some time. Remember, you don't want to be bogged down doing the heavy lifting.

My recommendation is that you start with two strategies and really focus on those strategies to make them work. There are no prizes for guessing that the first item on the agenda should be your web site. Remember, the web site is the doormat to your business. Most prospective clients will check out your web site before they have that initial meeting with you. A good web site will set things up nicely for that meeting. Along with that web site you should have a presence on the social media circuit. There are a number of platforms here. My preferred social media platform is LinkedIn.

In determining your positioning strategies you must also consider attending seminars and workshops. In order to grow your practice you need to grow your knowledge. The best way to learn marketing skills is to learn from the best. With most courses you can chalk up your professional development hours (required by professional bodies in order to maintain qualified status).

I have made mention of the Seven Drip Theory in this book. And here is my Seven Drip Theory for successful networking...

1. Mingle amongst the crowd and introduce yourself to people. When they ask what you do...deliver your elevator pitch. Collect cards from those people who show interest in your elevator pitch. These people are your target market. When you receive their card, make some notes on the card for future reference. Never give anyone your card unless they ask for it. That is Networking Etiquette. There is a reference at the end of this chapter to a great book on networking by Jennifer Harwood - essential reading.

2. Assuming the event is in the evening. The absolute first thing you do the next morning is to follow up on the business cards that you collected at the event. Remember the earlier your follow up the better your chances of conversion. The contact is not made by phone, it is made via Eyejot. This is a brilliant piece of software that allows you to send an email message. And the good news is that it is available free. The link is in the recommended resources at the end of this chapter. And here are the steps for success:-
    -   Set up EyeJot
    -   Make sure you look professional! Wear a similar colour shirt so they can recognise you from the night before!

- Have your notes handy so you can relate to them AND build RAPPORT, if you have no RAPPORT you will unlikely convert!
- Rehearse beforehand to ensure that you know exactly what you want to say
- Keep it under 30 seconds, make your point and make an impact!

During the Call:-
- Make sure you address them by first name (more personal), smile, look excited, you want them to be excited about what you have to offer!
- Bring up something from when you met them at the networking event- from the notes you made on their card
- Allow an opportunity to let them call you BUT just in case they don't, drop the 'I will call you next Monday for a catch up.' This will let them know you will be calling.

3. Follow up Phone call
    - This phone call is to further build rapport. If there is no rapport, terminate the process as you will unlikely convert. Remember we have no time to waste on Wood Ducks.
    - If rapport is there, arrange to give them access to your weekly 'Ask the Expert' calls.
    - The purpose of this call, once rapport has been developed, is to organise a screen share meeting.
    - If they would like more information about what you do then arrange time for a screen share or one-on-one meeting.

4. LinkedIn Connection
   Send a personal invitation to connect on LinkedIn and mention your earlier phone call.

5. Send the client a link to some information that you have on the area of expertise where they were showing some interest.

6. Screen Share
   - The purpose of the screen share is to find out more about the prospects business
   - In order to do so we will ask them questions about their business. Prepare a questionnaire prior to the call. Ensure there are some questions that they can't answer.
   - Offer to email some information on the topics they show particular interest in.

7. Close the Deal
   - Explain how you are different to all other accounting firms.
   - Offer a complimentary one-on-one consultation where the prospect can ask questions about their business and also about the benefits of appointing you as their accountant.
   - Arrange a meeting to discuss your menu of services and close the deal.

To summarise the Step-By-Step Process:
- Make a list of positioning strategies

- Prepare a budget for the positioning process

- Set aside some time for positioning and record this in your calendar

- Just do it

HOW IT WORKS

Positioning yourself and your business will differentiate you from your competition. Positioning means that you don't have to compete on price. Competing on price is competing to get to the bottom first.

You can have some fun positioning your Professional Knowledge Firm. There is a better chance of prospective clients coming through your door if you position yourself properly. There are a number of ways you can position yourself and you must select the strategies that best suit your personality and the way you do business. Marketing these days is all about people out there finding you, not you finding them. The days of door knocking are long gone, thank goodness.

There are still times when we have to use the old fashioned methods of burning shoe leather so to speak and visiting a number of prospects. Business people are time poor nowadays. They don't have time to look up telephone directories or read newspapers to find what they want. The first thing they do is go straight to the computer and tap into Google and that is why you need to position yourself with your web presence in order to give prospective clients every opportunity to find you.

So it makes sense, that if the majority of your target market is looking for you on Google, you must have a website that will stand out from the crowd and give them a reason to contact you. Your website will be more attractive to busy people if it has some videos explaining what you do. Some people would much rather look at the video than read reams of text in order to find out more information.

There are a number of ways to position your practice. And

it is not all about networking and attending functions. Before you get out there and start networking you need to have some form of profile to attract people to you. If you are positioned with a book, then people will want to talk to you. People need to be intrigued and find you interesting before they want to engage in conversation with you. With good positioning, you don't have to talk about the products and services that you offer; all you need to talk about is the benefits of dealing with your business. Remember your elevator pitch.

Selling is hard for accountants. It is not something that is included in their tertiary education or while working for an employer. So in order to become the head marketing person for your business you will need to attend some courses, seminars and workshops in order to learn these skills. Engage a mentor that can guide you through this process. The main thing you will learn from mentors and marketing courses is the art of selling without selling.

Whether you like it or not, if you want to grow your Professional Knowledge Firm, you need to get out and prospect. You are no longer in the business of providing professional services; you are now in the business of prospecting. And even though you have to be technically good at what you do, you cannot just rely on being technically good to grow your business. If people aren't coming in your door you just don't have a business. It is as simple as that. You can be the best technician in the world, but if you can't get people through the door you will go broke tomorrow. Once you have clients in the door, you can then work on referrals and testimonials to build your business, but you need to get them in the door first. This is called lead generation.

Positioning your firm will make it easy for people to find you. And when they do, you need to express the benefits of dealing with your firm. Talking about the process and how you do things will just send them to sleep. In order to keep your clients, you have to provide great service. In order to get the people in the door to find out how they can benefit from your ability, you need to position yourself. It is as simple as that.

To summarise how it works:

- Positioning will separate you from the pack.

- Positioning will allow potential clients to find you, rather than you having to find them.

WHY IT WORKS

The good thing about positioning is that you do not have to develop great selling skills in order to attract and convert potential clients to your business. Professionals are not skilled at selling. As a matter of fact they suck at it. So when professionals are trying to sell, they don't really feel all that comfortable. And when we don't feel comfortable, we don't perform well.

BE DIFFERENT

Positioning your business will save all the heartbreak of trying to convert prospective clients into customers. By doing all the work behind the scenes to differentiate yourself from your competitors, you will have prospective clients contacting you and asking you questions, instead of the reverse.

Once you have positioned your accounting practice, the networking game is made easy. Let's take for example the situation where you have written a book. Once you have written a book you have something to give away. And you are now an authority on the particular subject. Being an authority makes you stand out amongst the crowd and you will be approached by a number of organisations to do presentations and write papers, which means more exposure for your business. And regarding the networking side of things, people will always make conversation with you by asking you questions about your book. With the book you are in a position to give something away for free. When somebody is showing interest in your book, you should organise to meet with them and take along a copy of your book as a present. This in itself is a great starter for your pre-eminence. With marketing in this day and age, you need to start the process by giving something away. And the trick of the trade here is to give away the inexpensive stuff. That makes sense doesn't it? You could also consider inviting them to your weekly 'Ask the Expert' calls.

To put it another way how much value would you get out of $100 worth of radio or magazine advertising? If you answered 'absolutely nothing' you are correct. Imagine if you gave away 20 books instead. For starters, the recipients will really appreciate the fact that you are gifting them something. Reciprocity is a big thing. And these people will reciprocate by reading some of the contents of your book. They may also reciprocate by attending your 'Ask the Expert' calls and inviting a colleague. With all this reciprocity you have not only increased your conversion potential for prospective clients, but you have also increased your retention ratio with existing clients.

Think about the value to your business of having five new clients per month from a marketing investment of $300 per month? And ...How does that work?

Well to give away 50 books it will cost you around $300. These recipients are very grateful for this gift from you and you are now in a position to ask a small favour. And that favour is to have a meeting with you. Let's assume that 20 of these grateful recipients agreed to have a meeting with you. How many of these recipients do you need to convert to recoup your investment of $300? I will leave you with the equation. In your calculation you must consider the lifetime value of your average client.

To Summarise Why It Works:

- Positioning can save you time and money.

- You do not have to be physically present in the entire selling process.

- You will be seen as an authority with the right positioning.

- Positioning is all about making it easier for your target market to find you. And when they find

you there is a good chance they are going to
want to buy something from you.

THE BENEFITS

In today's market there are many inexpensive tools
available to you in order to position yourself and your
accounting practice. There are also a number of
outsourcing services available to assist with the marketing
process, including your social media exposure.

When you take the time to position yourself and your firm
properly your target market will find you and will come to
you. And that is what the game is all about. The days of
making cold calls and burning shoe leather are well and
truly gone.

Once you have defined your target market and ideal client
all that needs to be done is to find out their pain and their
fear in dealing with accountants. And then you interrupt
them by entering the conversation going on inside their
heads, and you do this via your web site, your yellow page
ad, the way you answer the phone at your office, and your
elevator pitch.

Positioning is like fishing. If you use the wrong bait you
won't get any bites. Use the right bait to attract the right
people. There are numerous networking groups and there is
no point in attending a group that is not interested in the
services you offer. What you need to do is find a group that
would benefit from the services you provide. For example,
there would be no point you joining an employee group
when your target market is small business. On the other
hand you could certainly consider joining a bookkeeping
group as they are dealing with your clients but in a different
perspective.

With LinkedIn Groups you must consistently offer support
by including comments and conducting surveys on a

regular basis. You must be active and you must give your knowledge without expecting anything in return.

Writing blogs is all part of the process and is another inexpensive way to position yourself in the market. Blogs can be written on your own platform and promoted through social media network, or you can write comments on the blogs of other business groups. Either way, your posts will contain information that will assist the members of the group. By consistently writing great blogs you will attract followers. It is important that you publish your blog on the same day and at the same time each week so that your followers know when they can find you. Set aside certain times throughout the week where you will make comments on various media sites. This is a great positioning tool as people involved in these groups will check your LinkedIn profile and will want to catch up with you to continue discussions and to learn more.

Imagine the cost of positioning yourself using radio or television advertising as your positioning tool. These are great tools for exposing your business, but you may run out of money before you get any results. You must be careful with this form of advertising to ensure that you do not attract clients outside your target market.

When you consistently work on your positioning you will create marketing momentum. Positioning has the effect of separating you from your competition. You will be giving people a reason to want your service offerings. The most important part of the marketing process is gaining rapport with your potential client. Offering your knowledge through social media and the publishing of books will reduce the time involved in the rapport-building process.

The other advantage of creative positioning is that it is inexpensive compared to other forms of advertising. You will also attract the type of clients that you want for your business.

TIP: You don't have to *be* the best technician in your profession to succeed. In order to succeed you have to position yourself and your firm to *look* like you are the expert. Being and looking are two very different things. Looking the part will get you more clients than being the part. Giving your clients exceptional service will ensure a high retention ratio.

CASE STUDIES

When it comes to professionals the larger firms are great examples of positioning, although they work more along the lines of branding rather than positioning.

There was one case where we clearly demonstrated the cost of using a time cost system. This particular accounting firm engaged us to conduct a workshop with our Cost of Time Costing program. This is an evaluation of the actual cost to the accounting firm in using a time cost system and the costs associated with billing clients on a time cost basis, as opposed to invoicing clients on a fixed price/ value pricing basis.

We went through the exercise with all partners present, asking a series of questions about time and costs associated with the system such as WIP write offs, debtor write-offs and the time taken to administer the system. We plugged the responses into our spreadsheet calculator and the actual cost of conducting the time cost system was calculated.

At the conclusion of this exercise our calculator showed that the costs associated with using a time based system represented over 18 percent of total revenue.

The partners made a decision there and then to trash the time cost system. This was a great positioning opportunity. They took this opportunity to update their web site and all other social media. They also had a good look at their menu of services and worked on ways to bundle service packages together.

They had now found a point of differentiation from other accounting firms in their area and they made sure that they drove this point home at every opportunity. They would have luncheons at their office once per month and invite prospective clients who wanted to learn more about how fixed pricing could benefit their business. The revenue of the firm increased by just under 23 percent within 12 months after their decision to position themselves as the fixed price accounting firm.

Action Steps to assist with the implementation of these Strategies:-

Your action plan to move forward on positioning:

- Make a list of all the positioning activities available.

- Attend seminars on social media presentation.

- Develop an elevator pitch.

- Attend networking events.

- Review your profiles on social media sites.

- Work on implementing two positioning activities per month.

- Engage an outsource service to distribute your blogs.

RECOMMENDED RESOURCES

'The Art of Networking' - Jennifer Harwood

'5 Simple Strategies to Market Your Business on LinkedIn' - Sally Z.C O'Connor
http://www.amazon.com/Strategies-Business-LinkedIn-Marketing-ebook/dp/B00BUX4GY2

'Facebook for Business Owners' - Tom Corson-Knowles
http://www.amazon.com/Facebook-Business-Owners-Businesses-ebook/dp/B009PPCPUE

'How to Create a Step-by-Step LinkedIn Marketing Strategy for Your Business' - Josh Turner
http://www.amazon.com/LinkedIn-Marketing-Strategy-Business-ebook/dp/B00AW1O1F2

'Secrets of SEO Marketing: Strategies on How I Learned to Get to the Top of Search Engines and How You Can Too' - Jimena Cortes: The link to her book is below:

http://www.amazon.com/Secrets-SEO-Marketing-Strategies-ebook/dp/B0067U72YE/

For more information on the "Cost of Time Cost Calculator," visit our web site at
www.businessdevelopmentspecialists.com.au

Eyejot software for sending video emails:-

www.eyejot.com

CHAPTER 4

Purchasing That Accounting Practice – How to Get the Best Return on Your Investment

THE STRATEGY

There are a number of ways to grow a Professional Knowledge Firm. For those impatient Generation Y types out there that want their professional firm NOW, there is a solution, and that solution is to buy an established business or purchase a block of fees. The advantages of buying a business is that you can also acquire premises (that are already set up) and also the team members associated with the business.

Purchasing of fees is not something I would always recommend as there are now so many inexpensive methods of growing an accounting practice without having to purchase fees. There are a number of pitfalls with buying fees so you have to enter this game with extreme caution. You must determine your plan of attack for the purchase and you need to negotiate and draw up water tight agreements. This is not a game for the faint hearted. During this process there are always a number of twists and turns that will require you to stop, re-negotiate, and go back to the drawing board.

The most important thing to remember with acquisition of fees is to give yourself an exit clause whereby you can recover most, if not all, of your deposit if things don't go your way.

The other thing that you must consider is the taxation implications of purchasing fees. I haven't been involved with taxation for some time now so you will have to discuss any taxation strategies with your adviser. Back in my tax days, the acquisition of fees, or the acquisition of a business, is a transaction of a capital nature and cannot be written off as an expense for taxation purposes. This means that say for example you purchase an accounting firm (or block of fees) for $200,000, you will not get a tax deduction for that transaction. After your acquisition you will run this accounting firm and (hopefully) derive fees of $200,000 in your first year (less expenses) and you will pay income tax on that net income.

On the other hand, if you spent $200,000 on marketing to generate $200,000 worth of fees, you would be able to claim the marketing expense as a tax deduction. Have a think about this alternative to purchasing professional fees. Think about the business you could build on a $200,000 (successful) marketing budget.

With the purchase of professional fees there are a number of dos and don'ts and also a number of traps for young players. This is a tough process, it's not just purchase the business and off we go. There is a bus load of work to be done to protect your investment and get the best return possible.

To Summarise the Strategy:

* Look at the alternatives to purchasing fees.

- Consider the tax implications regarding your acquisition.

- Do you purchase an established practice or a block of fees?

- Negotiate hard and draw up water tight legal documents with an exit clause.

TIP: Think about the fees you could generate from a marketing campaign of equivalent value to the acquisition cost.

THE STEP-BY-STEP PROCESS

Let's assume you are going to purchase an established accounting practice. And let's assume that the fee base for this practice is $500,000. The sale price for this business is $500,000, i.e. the vendor wants dollar for dollar, which is pretty much stock standard. We are also assuming here that the fee base does not include any income from financial planning. That is a different story again, and complicated. So for the purpose of the exercise we will keep it simple.

There will likely be an agent involved in the transaction. So the first thing you will do is gather some details from the agent about the fee base. You should ensure that you obtain the following information:-

a) Verify value of fees

b) Number of clients in total

c) Number of employees

d) Employee records

e) Provision for annual leave and Long Service Leave for employees

f) Mix of employees between administration and professional

g) Work In Progress (WIP) listing

h) Debtor listing

i) Number of clients - fee range $0 to $500

j) Number of clients - fee range $500 to $2,000

k) Number of clients - fee range $2,000 to $5,000

l) Number of clients - fee range $5,000 to $10,000

m) Number of clients - fee range $10,000 to $20,000

n) Number of clients - fee range above $20,000

o) Menu of services detailing all service offerings

p) Does the firm operate on time billing or fixed pricing?

q) If time billing, how many clients are on fixed price agreements?

r) Does the firm provide business consulting services?

s) WIP write off for previous three years

t) Debtor write off for previous three years

u) Revenue per partner

v) Software packages

w) Standard of IT

x) Value of furniture and fittings

y) Details of lease on premises

z) Are any of the partners willing to stay on after the acquisition?

By asking for all this information you are commencing your process of elimination. If the vendor cannot provide all this information you have to tread with caution. On the other hand, as long as you are provided with the most important information, you may be in a position to negotiate a little harder.

Once you have received all this information, you must then do your due diligence and in doing so you need to make up a long list of questions. The more questions you ask at the initial interview the more chance you have of unsettling the vendor. There may be some questions that the vendor should have been asking himself, or herself. All you need to do here is to create some element of doubt in the vendor's mind.

The next step is to get ready for the meeting with the vendor with all your questions and agenda prepared.

During the course of your due diligence you may find that you come across items that do not necessarily tick all of your boxes. That's okay as you can bring these items to the meeting and commence the process of negotiation, starting with the price of the business. You should take these items into account and have a set figure in mind for the purchase of the business and this figure is based on your return on investment. If the vendor will not budge on price then you need to bring some items to his/her attention that will make them more flexible with the price negotiation. If the vendor is a hard head, then I would advise that you exit the negotiations and let someone else waste their time with the acquisition.

The vendor can most times be a pretty good indication of the nature of the client base... Birds of a feather often flock together. You may decide early in the piece that you don't really want to buy this business. You must also consider the price you would be prepared to pay for this business and go from there. Work on a strategy that will convince the vendor that their business is worth less than what they believe it to be and back this up with evidence. You need to get as much of this out of the way before you part with your deposit.

In most cases you will have to pay some form of deposit before you are allowed near the client base. The negotiation starts before you pay your deposit and you must have a water tight agreement that gives you an exit clause should you decide that it is not feasible to proceed. You should also ensure that most (if not all) of your deposit will be refunded. You must also insist that the deposit is held in a trust fund awaiting your approval for release, whether it is the agent's trust fund or your solicitor's trust fund.

The contract should be split up into stages, based on your negotiations, with a certain amount of funds to be released at each stage of the acquisition process. The name of the game is to pay as little money as possible in order to get to meet the client base.

Once you have agreed on the terms of the contract, it is then time to meet with some of the clients, firstly to make sure they exist and secondly to make sure you want them as clients. Prior to these meetings you will have to set out a game plan and you should have a number of questions for the client that will allow you to determine whether they fit with your definition of ideal client.

You need to take your menu of services into those meetings and you also need to discuss fixed price agreements with the clients to get a feel for their opinion on this. Also to get some confirmation that they are comfortable with a fixed price intend coming on board with that system.

This will also give you an indication as to whether there is scope for increasing fees. In order to get the best out of these meetings it is important that you are aware of the fees that the clients paid in the previous three years and the full details of the services provided in relation to those fees. There may be some cases where fees have been derived on a one-off basis or in relation to the acquisition of a business or a tax investigation. You need to know the nature of the client's business and ensure that it is not dirty.

The goal is to see as many of the clients as possible, particularly the top 20 percent of fee earners. It is very likely that this top 20 percent will represent 80 percent of the fee base. You must have a very clear picture of what you want out of this acquisition. You may only want to take on the clients that are business owners. You then need to determine what you want to do with the remaining clients. You may want to bundle these clients and sell them off as a block of fees to another professional who can best service their requirements.

We will have a look at some strategies for on-sale of fees in the How it Works segment.

To summarise the step-by-step process:

- Determine what you want from the acquisition.

- Calculate what you are prepared to pay for the business based on return on your investment.

- Do the hard and fast negotiations before paying a holding deposit.

- Prepare a plan of attack for the negotiations.

- Have your solicitor ensure that the contract is water tight.

- Ensure the contract for sale has an exit clause that ensures that you will be refunded most, if not all, of your deposit should the deal fall through.

TIP: Negotiate the price and the terms of the contract before you proceed with the payment of a deposit. Always have an exit clause in the contract.

HOW IT WORKS

With the purchase of any business you must look at the deal in the eyes of the vendor. I can guarantee you that the vendor is keen to sell the business and wants to move on. As a matter of fact, the vendor will be keener to sell than you are to buy, so bear this in mind in your negotiations. You need to play hard ball because you are in the box seat.

In most cases, where a vendor is selling a business, their decision to sell has been made too late. By too late, I mean they have decided to sell when they have had enough of the business and don't want to be there anymore. And this has been the case for some time prior to offering the business for sale. This attitude is generally reflected in the figures.

By the time most vendors decide to sell it is too late. They are sick and tired of the business, probably caused by a few setbacks, and they really don't want to turn up anymore. This vendor is ready to do a deal. They just want to get out and they want to exit as quickly and as cleanly as possible and will be prepared to reduce their price or allow some terms in order to do so.

You need to arrange the purchase of the business in four tranches. The first will be the deposit. The deposit should be held in a trust account, not to be released without *your* authority. You must endeavour to make the initial deposit as small as possible. Try to work on five percent. This deposit will get you a look at the client listing so that you can complete your due diligence. Before commencing your due diligence on the client base you need to work out what type of client you want to buy. At this stage it is important for you to have a clear definition of your ideal client.

You also have to be clear on the type of client that you don't want. You may say you don't want any client with a fee of less than $2,000 per annum. But have another think about this. If you are going to be providing financial planning services then there may well be the potential to increase the fees for those clients that pay less than $2,000 per annum. So make sure you think about the potential of the client base first.

If you have determined that you don't really want to take on any client with an annual fee of less than $2,000 then you can approach the vendor and request that these clients be excluded from the sale. I think it is highly unlikely that the vendor would want to accept this proposal. Looking at the situation from his/her point of view, he/she is now confronted with selling the practice in two parts and all he/she wants to do is to walk away. This strategy was just a thought and you can try it on if you want to save a few bucks on the purchase and reduce the administrative process at the same time. You don't ask...you don't get.

Let's assume that you have no alternative but to buy the entire business. In other words, you have to take the good with the bad. But you know what, it ain't that bad. Have a think about what you could do with the client population that pays less than $2,000 in fees per annum. There could be some massive potential here for additional services such as financial services, including insurance and finance. And you never know, some of these clients may have family or know people that actually fit into your definition of ideal client. I will discuss this in more detail in the Why It Works segment of this chapter.

Once you have decided that you want to proceed with this acquisition, it is then time to negotiate the terms of the contract. You will need to stump up a sizeable deposit in order to meet with the clients. This is the point of no return for the vendor. The point at which he/she has to notify their clients they are moving on. You need to negotiate a deposit of *no more* than 25 percent. You have already paid a five percent deposit to look at the client listing, now you have to come up with a further 20 percent to have a look at the stock. If the vendor wants more than 25 percent for this next stage, then you could offer to release 10 percent of the deposit to them. You need to ensure that you are not going to part with too much money just to find out that the client base is not your cup of tea.

As part of your initial due diligence you will be able to check out the web sites for most of the clients in order to get a feel for the value. So before you part with an additional 20 percent of hard earned cash you can form some sort of opinion from your due diligence.

In order to complete your due diligence at stage one, you should have been provided with a list of all the clients and the annual fees that they paid for the last three financial years. You need to sequence this list in order of highest to lowest. Take the top 20 percent from this list and add up their fees. It will very likely turn out they are contributing 80 percent or more of the total fee base. So, if the vendor is wanting more than 25 percent down before he introduces you to the client base, you need to negotiate on the basis that you only want to visit a small population of the client base. You may only be visiting 20 clients, but these clients could represent say 60 percent of the fees. As long as you can ensure that this client population will come on board, then you have made ground on reducing the risk of the purchase.

Another item that helps keep the vendor honest is the claw back clause in the contract. I will not go into much detail here as this is a stock standard clause in accounting practice sale contracts. It basically states if the purchaser does not derive at least 70 percent of the fees as per the contract, then the vendor will reimburse the purchaser for the shortfall. So make sure you negotiate this claw back percentage as high as possible and keep it in a trust account until you authorise the release.

In order to explain this concept, let's look at our current situation. You could negotiate a claw back clause of say 80 percent, which means that the vendor is to reimburse you dollar for dollar of any shortfall (over 80%) in the fees you derive from this client base over the next 12 months. Assuming the purchase price is $500,000, then the claw back clause would mean the vendor reimburses the purchaser dollar for dollar for any shortfall under $400,000. So, if the purchaser derives only $300,000 from this client base over the next 12 months, then the vendor will reimburse $100,000 (assuming the purchaser paid dollar for dollar for the fee base). I would suggest that the vendor be drip fed with payments on a quarterly basis. Release a minimum amount to the vendor upon exchange of contracts. Have the remainder of the settlement held in deposit and release amounts from that deposit on a quarterly basis in accordance with the fees that have been derived from the client base during that quarter.

As a purchaser you may be thinking that if you delay the receipt of fees that you will be in front. That is not only dishonest, it is just plain dumb, and any purchaser trying this on will go broke doing so.

Your goal as purchaser is to make the most out of this client base. The first step in this process (after settlement) is to meet with every one of the clients you are purchasing, and do so as soon as possible. You need to set a plan to ensure this process is completed in less than three months from settlement. The main reason for having these meetings is to verify that the clients actually exist. From this enquiry you may ascertain that some clients no longer exist or will not be continuing as a client for some reason or another. Once you have verified the number of clients coming on board, you need to inform the vendor. If there are a material number of clients that have verified they are no longer a client of the business, you need to inform the vendor and negotiate a reduction in price. This is also a good lead up to negotiating an early reduced final settlement. You are putting some element of doubt in the vendor's mind in relation to the value of the practice and that will assist with negotiations on the final price that you pay.

Before you meet with the client base, you must have a strategy together for the meetings. There will obviously be different strategies for different groups i.e. there will be a different strategy for business owners, one for investors, and one for individuals. Before meeting with these clients you will need to have your menu of services and a script, including a questionnaire. And the best thing to do is to start from the top and work your way down.

At the meetings with the business clients, you will discuss your menu of services. The goal here is to find out the needs and wants of these business owners and then put together a bundle of services for them. In order to do this you will have to put together some questions for these clients. By asking questions you will be giving them the opportunity to tell you what they want and for them to indicate their expectations from you.

You will also have to advise them of the way you do business, i.e. that you have fixed price agreements with your clients, the benefits of having a fixed price agreement, and why time cost billing is not good value for them. You should also take this opportunity to agree on a price for the next 12 months. By the time you have finished the interviews with all the business clients, you will have a much clearer picture of the how things are going to pan out for the next 12 months. There will be some business owners who do not want to go on to fixed pricing. That's ok. You can still do work with these clients and have a plan to work on them over the next 12 months to convert them to fixed pricing. Just run with these clients for at least 12 months and recover your cost of acquisition and then you can decide the best option for them. This will be dealt with in more detail in chapter 9.

When you have finished with the business clients you need to then work with the individuals. There are a number of packages you can work on with individuals and again you will have to compile a questionnaire in order to ascertain their needs and wants. This is a great opportunity to talk to them about wealth creation and the reason why income protection and other insurances are an important part of reaching financial goals. Your questions will also give you a clear picture of the level of service that they have been receiving from the vendor. If these clients have only been coming in once a year to get their tax returns completed, then there is great potential to provide additional services, to bundle these services, and to put together a fixed price agreement. And the best way to start the new relationship is to offer them a complimentary financial health check with your financial planning division, i.e. your outsourced financial planner. Giving something away for free is a nice way to start a relationship.

From the interview process there will be some clients that indicate that they have no intention of continuing on with you (or the firm) as their adviser. You need to find out why because in some instances they may indicate that they were already in the process of moving to another advisor and had informed the vendor. You need to deduct these clients from the purchase price.

Remember, the vendor is tired of the practice, and sometimes this shows in the quality of the work. Compile a list of these clients that have indicated that they will not be proceeding and go into negotiation with the vendor about the real value of the business. Remember, you need to create that element of doubt about the value of the practice based on cold hard facts. There is no point paying dollar for dollar fees for a client that is not going to continue with the firm. The valuation for the business is based on the value of the fee base.

Let's look at an example here to clarify. Using our model, the purchase price for this business is $500,000 and that price is calculated as the dollar for dollar value of the fee base. You interview the client base and come up with the following information:

- Five of the business clients have indicated that they were already in the process of moving to another adviser. Value - $50,000.

- There were 30 individual clients that could not be contacted as they have moved or no longer exist. Value - $25,000.

- There were 10 clients that had a one-off service during the year, for example, a tax investigation or insurance claim. These are unusual items and not part of the clients' normal annual fee. The fee for one-off situations has to be deducted. Value - $40,000. This is the reason why you ask to see the fees that have been derived from the clients for each of the last three years. This information will expose these abnormalities.

As a purchaser you are paying for fees that you will be deriving from the clients of this business over the next 12 months. And to substantiate this value, you are given a list of clients with their dollar value (or standard fee revenue) shown next to their name. From your interviewing process you have ascertained that there is an amount of $115,000 that you will not be able to recover in fees from this client base, so the price on the contract of sale has to be amended to reflect the true value or purchase price of the practice. You need to nip this in the bud early and your contract should allow for adjustment of the price after initial contact with the client base. There is a great case study at the end of this chapter that will clarify how this works.

To summarise how it works:

- You need to verify the true value of your acquisition.

- Verify the existence and value of the client base by the interview process.

- Be prepared for every interview with questions and a script.

- Your questionnaire will identify the wants and needs of the clients.

- Work out who's coming and who's not and renegotiate the purchase price for the practice.

TIP: There is no point paying for something that you are not going to receive. Find out the true value of your acquisition as soon as possible.

WHY IT WORKS

It is important that you conclude your due diligence process as soon as possible. The final part of your due diligence process is to verify:

➢ That the clients exist.

➢ That the value shown for the client is recoverable.

You won't be able to meet with the client base until you have released some funds to the vendor. Releasing as little as possible initially will leave the door open for some negotiation on adjustment of the price and possible early settlement.

It is important that you prepare for each of these interviews, especially with the high fee business clients. This is your opportunity to ask questions to find out their needs and wants, and then to introduce your menu of services and discuss the benefits of doing business with you and also the benefits of having a fixed price agreement in place. The questions that you will be asking the client in the interview should lead into this discussion.

By discussing a fixed price agreement with the client up front you will have a clearer picture of the fees that you will derive from that client over the next 12 months. It is highly likely that the fixed price agreement for the next 12 months will be for more money than they paid in fees to the vendor in the previous 12 months, and that is because you are offering more services and better value to the client and they are prepared to pay for that. With the initial interview process you should be able to increase the value of the fee base, especially for those business clients.

By interviewing the client base straight away you will have the opportunity to introduce yourself and your team. Bear in mind that most of the clients will be apprehensive about the change. You need to eliminate any element of doubt as soon as you can. The longer you put off that initial interview, the longer the client has to think about their options. Put yourself in the clients' shoes. You receive a letter or email stating that you have a new accountant and then you don't hear anything for six months. Would you be wondering if they care about you? Would you be wondering if the purchaser is a bit of a rooster? And would you be wondering about taking the opportunity to move on to another accountant, maybe someone that you know?

The other danger you face in not meeting the client base in a reasonable amount of time is that some clients may defect and the vendor can blame you by saying that they would have stayed had you communicated with them. By arranging introductory meetings quickly you will know exactly what you are buying and will be able to renegotiate the purchase price should clients confirm that they will not be staying with the business and for whatever reason. You need to keep your negotiating position in the best possible shape at all times. There are, unfortunately, some vendors that overstate the value of fees charged in the previous year. The interview process will identify this.

The other advantage of meeting early with the clients is that you can start working with them and start deriving income and getting some return on your investment. Your goal with the business clients is to get all of them on fixed fees. The case study at the end of this chapter will show why this works. And you need to focus on that top 20 percent because I'll bet you London to a brick they represent 80 percent of the total fee base.

By implementing fixed pricing with the clients and bundling in some additional services, you will be able to increase the fee base. The clients are happy to pay more as long as they can see the value (we have heard this so many times through our Client Engagement Review process. More details about this in chapter six).

Let's say the top 20 percent of the clients in the vendor business represent 80 percent of the fee base. In our example, this figure would be $400,000. If you interviewed this top 20 percent and negotiated a fixed price agreement which results in your fee being 15 percent higher than what they paid the previous year, you would have increased the value of this sector by $60,000; a bonus for you. So, by meeting with these clients and confirming that they will be staying on with you, and further confirming what they will be paying you (minimum), you have eliminated a fair amount of risk in the deal. Does that make sense?

You are probably thinking right here and now that this all looks too easy. It's not easy, you have to put in the hard yards to make this work and the hard yards are what put you in a great position to negotiate and renegotiate. I have seen some business acquisitions that have gone seriously wrong due mainly to lack of communication between the parties and because the purchaser did not have a plan to make the best out of the acquisition and, in doing so, reduce as much risk as possible. I have seen purchasers ripped off by unscrupulous vendors and vendors ripped off by unscrupulous purchasers. You need to have a plan in place and be on your best game to ensure this doesn't happen to you.

As part of your due diligence process you will be provided with a list of clients that you will be acquiring with the business, and the fees that they paid in the previous 12 months. You must insist that the fees for the previous three years are shown on this list. Let me tell you why.

There will be a number of cases where there are one-off services performed for the client. As the name implies, these services are a one-off and not usually charged to the client e.g. forensic accounting involved with a court case, a tax audit or even the acquisition of another business. If there were fees charged for the sale of their business you have a pretty fair indication that they will not be paying fees in relation to accounting services for that business over the next 12 months as it doesn't exist. By obtaining as much information as possible you reduce your risk factor with the acquisition. You may also find things that could result in you not proceeding with the acquisition; things that could give you an exit from the deal with a full refund.

By looking at the fees charged to the client over the last three years you can detect any abnormalities or big increases in fees in the third year. And this third year is the year on which your purchase price will be based. The fees paid in this year are the fees that are used to value that particular client and the overall value of the purchase. So if you are paying for something, you need to make sure you are getting value.

Let's take for example you notice a client on the listing who was charged $5,000 the first year, $7,000 the second and $25,000 in the third. This is what I would call abnormal and you need to discuss this with the vendor and find out the reason for the jump in fees. If the fee of $25,000 included an amount of $15,000 for a one-off tax audit, then you need to deduct this one-off fee in considering the value of that client to you over the next 12 months. The value for this client will then need to be reduced by $15,000 and accordingly, the purchase price will have to be adjusted by that same amount. Can you see here how you can reduce your cost of acquisition and at the same time place some element of doubt (in relation to value of the business) in the mind of the vendor? This element of doubt is important for final settlement negotiations.

The claw-back clause in a contract of sale for a professional firm is there as a buffer in case everything goes pear shaped. Let me tell you, from my own experience, you don't want to get tied up in an argument over the claw-back clause. That is why I have recommended that if you purchase an accounting practice or block of fees you work out very quickly which of the clients are going to stay, and, of the clients that are going to stay, determine the fees that you will be deriving from them over the next 12 months. Once you have a clear picture here it is time to go back and settle the contract prior to the due date and negotiate a discount for early settlement.

The only way to find out the value of your acquisition is to meet face to face with every one of the clients purchased as soon as feasibly possible. Once you have completed this exercise you are then in a position to go back to the vendor and advise of all the clients that have indicated that they are not coming on board. You are now in a position to negotiate the final settlement of the fee base. And what you need to do is create some uncertainty in the mind of the vendor. The best way to do this is to go through the list of clients with the vendor and show him/her the clients that have indicated to you that they will not be requiring any accounting services from the practice in the coming 12 months. There may be some cases where the client informs you that they had already notified the vendor that they had moved to another adviser. And you need to mention this to the vendor and suggest they check their lodgement listing to see if there are any more of these.

When you present that list to the vendor you also need to show the value of those fees that will not be coming in the door next year. It is at this point that you need to suggest to the vendor that you have some concerns about meeting the percentage agreed on the claw-back clause in the contract. You could also put a proposal to the vendor to reduce the purchase price of the business, and in doing so you are prepared to settle this matter now (being nine months before final settlement date) and in addition to that, you would be prepared to release the remaining funds held in trust to complete the matter. Remember what was mentioned previously. The vendor is much keener to sell than you are to buy and if you offer an early exit from the practice so they can wipe their hands of the deal, they will be all ears. I will demonstrate how this works in the case study at the end of this chapter.

The other good thing about buying an established accounting practice is that you have a database that you are deriving fees from almost immediately. You can work off this database to get even more clients through your referral process and marketing. The goal here is to double the fee base of the business in less than 24 months.

To summarise why it works:

- You need to determine the value of your acquisition.

- Meet with every client on the purchase list to verify they exist.

- Gather information from the client list and prepare a proposal for discount and early settlement.

TIP: Act swiftly on meeting the client base. Don't let the passing of time kill a good deal.

THE BENEFITS

One of the benefits of acquiring an accounting practice is that you have a ready-made database. You have a premises already fitted out and you have team members that can assist you with the transition.

You will also derive income immediately. You have the opportunity of verifying the value of your purchase and also the opportunity of reducing the purchase price if you act quickly in verifying the worth of the practice through extensive due diligence.

By meeting with every client on the purchase list you have the benefit of discussing your menu of services and the relationship with them going forward. At these meetings you also have the opportunity to discuss fixed price agreements for the next 12 months and the benefit here for the client is that they know exactly what they will be paying in accounting fees for the next 12 months and they are comfortable with the value that they will be deriving from the fees. This is also your opportunity to increase the value of the fee base.

In negotiating the terms of the contract it is important that you meet with the top 20 percent of the clients—as determined by their fees—and get a clear indication that they will continue with the practice. This will reduce your risk in relation to the purchase. The reason for this is that this 20 percent of clients will very likely represent more than 80 percent of the total fee base. If any of these clients indicate that they will not continue with the business after the sale, you must discuss this with the vendor immediately and negotiate the deduction of these fees from the purchase price of the practice.

Before the vendor will agree to introduce you to any client, he or she will require some form of financial deposit and will require access to this deposit. By meeting with the top 20 fee producers, you will likely be doing your due diligence on around 80 percent of the total fees. This process will give you a fair indication of the return on your investment in the practice.

The benefits from requesting a list of clients fees derived over the previous three years is that you can quickly identify any abnormal fees they may have paid; fees for things such as court matters or even attending to a tax audit. Any abnormal fees must be reduced from the purchase price. By addressing these issues early in the negotiation process you can save a lot of time and money and if agreement can't be reached you have spent very little time and very little money in order to determine the valuation of the practice.

By moving quickly on the client base, you are taking control of the negotiation process. By meeting with each of the clients within three months of the acquisition, you will reassure clients that you are there to give them value. There is nothing worse than clients wondering what is going to happen with their new accountant. You need to get out there and tell them the value that you bring to the table. Your carefully planned questionnaires will gather information from the clients of their needs, desires and expectations. This gives you another opportunity to offer more services to the client and therefore derive more fees. Meeting with them will also help you determine which clients will not be coming on board. You will also have a good indication of the fees that you can derive from the remaining client base over the next 12 months.

Once you have met with the clients and compiled a list of those clients that are not proceeding, you can put a value on this defection and then approach the vendor to negotiate a reduced purchase price. By having a contract that keeps the vendor in the picture for the next 12 months, you are in a great position to negotiate a reduced price by offering the vendor an early release from the existing contractual obligations. Purchasing an accounting practice is no different to any other purchase. If you were purchasing a property, prior to the purchase you would be doing your due diligence to confirm the value of the property. You would be looking at the potential value of the property after some renovations. You would be looking for reasons to reduce the price of the property and presenting reasons to the vendor to place an element of doubt in their mind as to the true value of the property.

By doing your homework, you will benefit from a reduced price for the business and you will also benefit from applying your skills in making the business more valuable.

To summarise the benefits:

- Determine the value of your acquisition.

- Arrange to meet the top 20 percent of the client base to cover 80 percent of your due diligence.

- Position yourself for negotiation by doing the hard yards and meeting with all the clients.

- Negotiate a contract that will allow for negotiation.

CASE STUDIES

There are a number of case studies involving the acquisition of professional service firms and I must say I have seen some real disasters in my time. I have seen some matters that have been taken to court with disastrous consequences for all parties concerned. So take that as a warning and ensure that your contract is watertight and that it gives you room for negotiation of price after you have conducted appropriate due diligence.

So let's talk about a recent case where I assisted with the negotiation and acquisition of an accounting practice.

For the purpose of this exercise we will be assuming an acquisition price of $750,000. The main purpose of the case study is to indicate the due diligence required in order to protect the investment.

My client noticed an accounting practice was for sale so the first thing I did was contact the sales agent and obtained as much information as possible regarding the practice. To obtain more information I had to sign a confidentiality agreement. From the information that we received, we were able to very quickly ascertain the value of the top 20 percent of the clients of the business. At this stage we had not been provided with a client listing, but we did have a list of a number of clients attached to the range of fees. After looking at this information, we decided to proceed further. The next step was to meet with the vendor. Prior to this meeting we compiled a questionnaire that would give the answers that would indicate whether it was worth proceeding any further. My client did not attend any of these meetings for a number of reasons.

There is a lot to be learned from meeting with the vendor. Firstly, you get to have a look at the premises. If the premises is dingy, dark and grubby there is a fair chance that the client base is much the same. And if the vendor is a dickhead there is a fair chance that the majority of the client base is much the same. This doesn't mean that you don't proceed any further. It just means that warning bells should be ringing.

From meeting with the vendor I was able to ascertain that they were keen to move on. I also sensed that there was some tension amongst the partners of the firm. It was a great start to our acquisition.

There were good signs indicating some advantages to proceed further into the negotiation process. I gave the agent a list of the information required in order to conduct my initial due diligence. The request for information included:

> A list of every client to be included in the sale of the business, including addresses.

> Fees paid by each of these clients in the previous three years.

> Sequencing of the client listing in order of highest fees to lowest fees.

> Categorisation of client list into business owners, high net worth individuals, companies and trusts.

> Work in progress listing including WIP write-off.

> Aged debtors listing, including debtor write -off.

> An indication on a scale of 0 to 10 as to the likelihood of the client continuing on with the practice after the sale.

In order to obtain this information, my client had to pay a 10 percent deposit in good faith. We negotiated that this deposit would be held in the agent's trust account and could not be released without the authority of the purchaser.

We also had an agreement drawn up to specify the commitment of the vendors in supplying information, and also to specify the commitment of the purchaser in relation to the client base. This agreement gave a degree of comfort to the vendors as it set out the rules for the initial part of the game.

We had the agent organise a meeting with the vendors at their premises. You may well ask why we would want to have a meeting on the vendor's premises. Well we wanted to have a look at the office set up. We needed to see where these guys lived and how they looked after the house. Did they operate out of some dark and dingy office in the back of some shops, or did they have a swish looking office with a welcoming feel about it? I explained to my client the importance of these things. The look and feel of the office can be a good indication of the client base. If you sleep with dogs you wake up with flees. A tardy, dark, dingy office will attract tardy, dark, dingy clients.

As it turned out, the office was just fine; it just needed some TLC and this also indicated to me that the partners were getting a little tired with the practice. This was another positive factor in our process of acquisition.

The vendors were reluctant to provide three years of figures for the client base so we explained why we needed these numbers and that we would not proceed without this information.

I explained to the vendors that we needed to see three years of numbers for each client in order to identify any abnormalities in fees charged from year to year in relation to one-off services provided to those particular clients.

From the listing of clients, we were able to ascertain where 80 percent of the fees were coming from. To do this we sequenced the list of clients in order of highest fees paid in the previous year to lowest fees paid. The list totalled around $750,000 so the number we were looking for was $600,000. This number represented 80 percent of the fees.

So we added the list of fees and drew a line under the client where the cumulative total equalled $600,000.

We wanted to find out the percentage of the client base that represented 80 percent of the total revenue. That's right; we were applying the Pareto Rule to the client base. The total number of clients on the list was 1,100. The number of clients representing 80 percent of total fees was 240. Bingo! This meant that 21.8 percent of the clients represented 80 percent of the revenue. There was an average fee of $2,500 per client in this grouping.

The remaining 860 clients represented total fees of $150,000 with an average fee of $174 per client; a lot of administration for $150,000. A majority of the client base were individual income tax returns. My client was not keen on taking over the smaller individual income tax returns as he was looking for business owners as clients.

We then sat down and discussed the alternatives in dealing with these individual income tax return clients. There were three alternatives:

1. We could negotiate with the vendor that these fees not be included in the acquisition and that they could sell them separately as a block of fees.

2. We could interview each of these clients to see whether there was any potential for increased fees, either through providing financial planning services or other services.

3. We could find an outsource tax preparation service to look after these clients.

As it turned out, the vendor did not want to separate these clients from the acquisition and therefore we had to work with alternatives two and three.

From our due diligence on the client base, we found that there were some good clients on the listing. From talking to the vendors we were able to ascertain that they did not provide value-add advisory services to their clients. They were just doing the compliance work, which included preparation of accounts and income tax returns. The vendors did not offer fixed fees to any of their clients, although they did indicate that a number of their clients had requested a fixed fee from time to time. So this meant that everything was invoiced on a time cost basis. There were some substantial WIP write-offs in the previous 12 months that would require explanation in the course of our due diligence.

There was a huge potential to increase the fee base of this practice through introducing the menu of services to each of these clients and offering much more service than they were currently receiving from the vendor.

My client had a financial planning division which meant they had a great opportunity to work on the 840 clients in the lower 20 percent of fees and to offer them a range of financial services.

I interviewed a number of businesses that specialise in the preparation of individual income tax returns, which meant that my client could outsource all the administration and form filling that would be required for these 840 clients and would make money from the outsourcing. We made sure that the tax outsourcing entity did not provide financial services and that all financial planning enquiries would be directed back to my client. When I put up this proposal to my client, he very quickly changed his mind about the total client base and could see some value in working with the individuals.

My client was then happy to proceed to the next step, and this is where the negotiations started. The next step was the preparation of the contract and setting out the rules for the acquisition. This is where the vendor had to show his/her hand by informing some of the clients that they were selling the practice.

As part of the process we arranged to meet the top 50 clients of the firm in order of annual fees paid. This came after hours of negotiation and my client had to part with some funds into the trust account for this to happen. This makes sense from the vendor's perspective because meeting with these clients means they were announcing they were selling up and moving on, if they hadn't already done so.

Some of these meetings were conducted at the clients' premises and some at the vendor's office. Meeting at the clients' premises gave us a better feel for the value of the client. We prepared for these meetings by putting an information pack together showing the range of services that their new accountant had on offer. The information pack also gave us some indication from the client that they would be interested in additional services such as value-add advisory services. We also prepared a questionnaire for the interviews to determine whether these clients could see the benefit from the services on offer in the menu of services and also whether they would like to have a fixed price proposal for these services. This cross-section of 50 clients represented over $250,000 in fees.

We got through these interviews in less than three weeks and there were three clients that indicated that they would not be staying on after the acquisition, for whatever reason. That was good information. The fees from these clients totalled $20,000 and these fees were immediately deducted from the purchase price. We were now looking at a purchase price of $730,000. So, that little exercise just made my client $20,000... a good start.

From interviewing the top 50 clients we were able to get a feel for those clients that wanted more services and would be happy to discuss our menu of fees in more detail, and, in particular, a fixed pricing package.

So, let's have a look at the stats at this point of the deal. We had interviewed the top 50 clients. These clients represented total fees of $250,000. Three of the clients interviewed indicated that they would not be staying on. This left 47 clients representing fees of $230,000. These clients indicated that they would be interested in the additional services on offer and this meant there was potential to increase this fee base by at least $46,000. So, in summary, we negotiated $20,000 off the price and created $46,000 in additional fees; a probable windfall of $66,000.

From this due diligence my client was happy to proceed to the next step. This is where I started to plant the seed in the vendors' minds that their practice was not worth as much as they had originally anticipated. I mentioned that three clients had already indicated that they would not be coming on board. This equated to six percent of the sample tested.

The starting negotiation price was now at $730,000 and this price was subject to our interviews with the remaining client base over a three month period. Our client had agreed to acquire the practice, it was just the purchase price that remained to be finalised. I won't bore you with the full details of the contract. We negotiated the contract with the vendors with a starting price of $730,000 subject to our due diligence on the remaining client base. In addition we negotiated a claw-back clause based on a 20 percent claw-back (normally 30 percent or more). This meant that any recovery from the fee base less than 80 percent would be reimbursed dollar for dollar.

My client topped up the deposit to 20 percent of the purchase price. We negotiated that 50 percent of this deposit would be released to the vendor in good faith. The contract, along with all our rules, was now signed and for the next three months we had to work feverishly to interview as many clients as possible from the vendor's client base. We prepared a number of questionnaires for the different classes of clients.

The questionnaires were designed to:-

1. Determine that the client was going to remain as a client of the purchaser.
2. Determine if the client had any potential for increased fees from the value-add advisory services on offer.
3. Determine whether the client was going to be in business for the next 12 months.

4. Ascertain that the fee to be derived from the client for the next 12 months would be at least equal to the fee that they paid to the vendor in the previous 12 months, i.e. the fee shown on the list of clients.

5. Confirm that the client was interested in looking at the additional services on offer.

6. Determine that the client was interested in going ahead with a fixed price agreement.

7. Agree on a fixed price agreement with the client for the next 12 months.

This is where we got down to the business end. I'll cut the story short and get to the results. Over the next three months my client was able to do the following:-

➢ Re-visited the top 50 clients (now 47) that were introduced to by the vendor.

➢ Arranged fixed price agreements with 40 of these clients and increased the fee base by over $50,000 from these 40 clients.

➢ There were four of us working on the interview process that focussed on the top 20 percent of fee earners. This meant we had to interview an additional 190 clients over the next three months. These 190 clients represented fees of $350,000. From this process there were just over 20 clients that indicated they were not proceeding. This represented fees of $80,000 and this amount was deducted from the purchase price.

Of the remaining 170 clients (representing fees of $270,000) we were able to negotiate fixed price agreements with the majority of these clients. The fee base in this client sector was increased by more than $60,000 with the negotiated fixed price agreements.

➢ With the remaining 860 clients we separated the business owners from the individuals. There were 30 small business owners in this group and the value of these 30 small business owners was $45,000. We arranged to meet with them. All these business owners indicated that they were willing to proceed and we negotiated fixed price agreements with them. Because of their value, we gave no choice. It was either fixed price agreement or nothing. We increased this fee base by over $8,000.

➤ Of the 830 individual clients remaining we sent out a notice that we were taking over the business, along with our menu of services for individual investors and salaried employees. We also included a questionnaire that would let us know:

  a) That they were coming on board.
  b) They wanted an interview with our financial planner.
  c) They are interested in investing.
  d) The details of their current investments.

From this group there were 180 that either indicated they would not be using our services over the next 12 months or just didn't respond to our enquiry. The value of this defection was just over $25,000 so we had this amount deducted from the purchase price as well.

From the interviews conducted with a majority of this group over the three month discovery period, we estimated a fee increase of more than $15,000 per annum.

➤ In the course of our due diligence we were also able to detect some fee abnormalities in the last 12 months for such things as tax investigations, negotiations regarding litigation matters etc.

We calculated the value of the fee overstatement for these abnormalities was in excess of $50,000 and this had to be deducted from the purchase price.

In summary:
1. From our due diligence we were able to verify the clients that intended to proceed.
2. We were able to deduct $155,000 from the purchase price.
3. We discovered and confirmed an increase in fees of more than $125,000 and the potential for more.

After the expiry of three months we went back to the negotiating table with the vendor. This was the point of no return for the vendor. From our meetings with the vendor we felt some dissention between the partners. One of the partners had agreed to stay on with my client for 12 months to assist with the transitioning process. The other partners were all keen to move on and were also keen to make a clean break from the firm with no lingering issues. Having sensed all that, I realized my client was in a favourable negotiating position.

From the three month discovery period we were able to create doubt in the minds of the vendors about the value of the practice. Over 200 clients had verified that they were no longer clients. We also discovered that two of the clients were in fact in the hands of an administrator. There was obviously no hope of deriving any fees from these clients for the next 12 months as they were out of business. The vendors were very embarrassed when we mentioned the two companies under administration; two companies they were trying to flog off to my client. The vendor was only embarrassed because we caught them out but that little oversight changed the whole game.

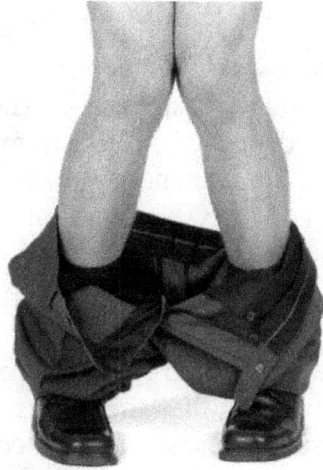

We caught 'em with their pants down...

My next question to the vendors was, 'Is there anything else you want to tell us, because if we find something down the track the next time we might not be so pleasant about dealing with it.'

I was now making it clear that we were going to agree on a final purchase price today and that final price had better not have any skeletons in the closet. Now that we were down to the pointy end on price, this sort of oversight could be seen as pure misrepresentation. We also mentioned the fee abnormalities that we had detected.

We now had to discuss the final purchase price and the remainder of the contract of sale details. The purchase price had already been reduced to $730,000 from our original findings. We now had evidence to reduce the purchase price by a further $155,000. This meant the starting negotiation purchase price was reduced to $575,000.

We then started negotiating the final purchase price. We started negotiating at $495,000. The final part of the negotiation was that we would rip up the original contract. We reminded the vendor that there was some false and misleading information attached to that contract and they might want to start over with a clean slate. I also indicated that my client was pretty pissed off that they tried to sell two clients that were in administration and, further, that I managed to convince him not to take that matter further with the authorities.

I also indicated that the remaining partner need not remain (we didn't want him anyway). We would not include any claw-back clause in the contract and the remaining deposit of $73,000 would be released to the vendor immediately, and the purchaser would pay the remaining agreed amount owing within 30 days. There would be no come-back on fees and this would be full and final settlement of the purchase. This meant that there was no need for the vendors to linger on. They could cut clean with their money and go their separate ways. It also meant that the settlement for the purchase of the business was brought forward by nine months. And when you divide the deduction from purchase price by the number of partners (three), the proposed deduction was a little easier to swallow.

The vendors could not wait to get away from each other. They would no longer be joined at the hip via this partnership. I had created an element of doubt and the vendors were also concerned that my client could detect further anomalies within the client base that could arise over the next nine months if the contract was drawn out full term. The vendors did not have enough faith in each other to be sure that there would be no more skeletons in the closet. The partner responsible for staying on would also be released from this task and could move on. This also meant that the other partners did not have to compensate this partner for staying on with the practice.

My client purchased the business for a total purchase price of $505,000. He also acquired some great team members along with established premises with no fit-out costs.

To summarise the outcome of this case study:

- The original purchase price of the business was $750,000.

- By carrying out thorough due diligence the price reduced to $505,000.

- By meeting with the business clients of the firm my client was able to increase the fee base by more than $125,000, with potential for more over the next 12 months.

- My client was in a great position to leverage off this fee base via their menu of services and other marketing strategies.

- Saving on purchase price - $245,000, plus a fee increase of $125,000. That adds up to a very tidy gain of $370,000.

- Minimum estimated return from fee base - $630,000 over the next 12 months.

So, I guess you want to know how the story ends? Well, over the next 12 months the purchaser (my client) was able to apply some marketing strategies and was able to increase the value of the client base. He increased the revenue to over $850,000 in the first 12 months. Not a bad return on a $505,000 outlay.

TIP: You need to position yourself for negotiation with thorough due diligence. The due diligence reduces the risk in the deal.

ACTION STEPS TO ASSIST WITH THE IMPLEMENTATION OF THESE STRATEGIES

Checklist for purchasing a business:

- Check the value of the business via thorough due diligence

- Get an idea of the value of this business by interviewing as many clients as possible

- Make sure the team members you are inheriting are good quality people

- Leave the door open for negotiation

- Create an element of doubt in the mind of the vendor in relation to the value of the business

- Always negotiate a due diligence period as part of the contract of sale

RECOMMENDED RESOURCES

"The 80/20 Principle" by Richard Koch
   http://www.amazon.com/The-80-20-Principle-Achieving/dp/0385491743

CHAPTER 5

Transitioning Your Clients to Fixed Price Contracts

How would you like to have an accounting practice that had:

- ✓ No work-in-progress.
- ✓ No debtors.
- ✓ No invoicing.
- ✓ Every client paying in advance and on the same day each month.

Have you ever asked your clients if they would prefer to be billed on a fixed price basis? We have (through our Customer Engagement Review process)... and the vast majority say yes.

There are more and more Professional Knowledge Firms that are billing their clients on a fixed price basis and they are attracting more quality clients (and quality team members) because of it.

This chapter is mainly aimed at those established accounting practices that are using time based billing. For those just starting out, this chapter will show you why you should *not* be conducting your practice using time based billing.

THE STRATEGY

I can already hear the 'yeah-buts' out there. You know, ' Yeah, but how do I account for time on a job?' 'How can I check on team productivity?'... I will answer that with a question.

How many times have you invoiced your clients for less than the amount shown on your WIP report because you didn't think the client got value, or because you thought the client would blow up if you rendered an invoice for that amount for the work performed?

That's right; it's all about value to the client and more than that, the client's perception of the value of the work performed. You must realise that clients don't care about price, they care about value. When a client refutes an invoice, you think they are arguing about price. WRONG... WRONG ...WRONG. The client is arguing about VALUE.

If you have stuffed up on a job and that stuff-up time is included on the timesheets, you wouldn't bill your clients for this time now would you? I hope not because I don't like crooks reading my books.

So, in almost all cases, your gut feeling will tell you how much the job is worth and you will ignore your WIP balance and bill the amount that your gut indicates is the right amount, i.e. the right value. And now, having completed this exercise, you have just wasted another hour thinking about it.

The big advantage of fixed pricing with your clients is that you get the money side of things out of the way upfront and then you can get on with doing the work and being more effective. Imagine all the time you would save in a year by not having heated discussions with clients about your fees being too high. It's not their fault. All they want is value and you are not explaining the value by showing them your time cost records.

You can create the perception of value in the client's eyes by going through your menu of services and explaining the benefits for them in relation to each of the services. They will then have the choice of the services that will best suit their needs and they feel they are getting some value. By going through the menu of services the client will better understand what you are doing for them. And when the clients profit from your value-add advisory services they won't mind paying you additional fees for this service as your fee is coming out of new profit and now your fee is actually seen as a smaller percentage of the profit your client is now deriving.

You could consider converting all your clients from time billing to fixed price agreements. You can hang on to your precious time cost system if you want, but you will soon realise how useless time costing is for everyone when you experience the change in productivity by billing your clients on a fixed price basis.

By transitioning your clients to fixed price contracts you will notice a marked increase in productivity and it is then you will realise how time costing is an inefficient model and filling out timesheets is a real time waster. Have a think about your own timesheet. How accurate are *your* monthly time sheets? Even if you have an electronic system that kicks in when you open the client file, you still have to mess around with the job codes and all that stuff. And what about when you are distracted and forget to turn the thing off? Then you have to go back in and reverse that time and try to remember how much time you really did spend. Bearing these factors in mind, now have a re-think about the accuracy of your time sheet. When it comes to invoicing the client you look at the WIP file and think, 'Did I really spend that much time doing that?' And you probably didn't. So, discretion is the better part of valour, and you write it off anyway. And besides that, you don't want to have that argument with the client.

Transitioning to fixed pricing will resolve all these issues for you. And your team members will be happier. This means that they don't have to sit down at the end of the week and work out who they are going to charge their time to so they can meet their productivity levels. Bullshit isn't it?

Efficiency, and more importantly effectiveness, can be measured very easily with fixed pricing. Did the job get finished on time? If not, why not? When the 'why not' is explained you can then work on making some changes to ensure that the job is finished on time. It may mean that the team member requires more training, or they need to go on a holiday for the rest of the year to think about it. Or maybe the client has caused the problem and we need to discuss a change order for the extra work that has to be performed to rectify the anomaly, should it occur again.

Your clients will soon let you know if you are not performing to their expectations of value. They have paid for the work and they want value for their money. And they want it done accurately and according to agreed time lines.

Fixed pricing also works when you outsource all your compliance work. You can get a fixed price quote from your outsource company. Once you have a fixed price for the compliance work it is then very easy to price the job for the client. Does that make sense?

To summarise the strategy for transition to fixed pricing:

- Come to the conclusion that time billing is not efficient, nor is it effective.

- You need to work out a plan for transitioning your clients from time billing to fixed price contracts.

- You need to work out the benefits for the client and get buy-in from the clients by conveying those benefits.

- Prepare a menu of services showing everything you do. The menu should have needs on one side and wants on the other. Clients buy what they want, not what they need and that is why it is important to separate the two.

- You need to put your proposal together before meeting with the clients.

TIP: Talk to your clients about fixed pricing before they discuss it with another accountant and decide to move on.

THE STEP-BY-STEP PROCESS

When you have made the decision to enter the 21st Century and introduce fixed pricing to your clients, there are some steps that you will need to take to ensure that the transformation runs smoothly. This will result in benefits for both you and your clients...win-win. Firstly, you need to write a strategic plan for the transformation. This will include checklists and questionnaires to ensure that everything is covered.

You will then need to prepare a menu of services. This is best done in a brainstorming session with your team members. They will know better than you what the clients are looking for in the way of services. There may be some team members willing to take over the challenge of introducing some new services that the practice can offer to their clients.

When you put together the menu of services remember to talk about the benefits to the clients. Your clients don't give a damn about the process, they just want to know the result and how the result benefits them.

Put together some service packages. You could start with the bronze service and then you could have silver, gold and platinum services. With all the service packages you must include all phone calls, meetings and emails. This means you will be differentiating these service packages from the service that you are currently delivering. The client won't be thinking about the fees they were charged last year when considering the price for the fixed price agreement because the service offering is completely different. You know and

I know that the service offering is very similar to last year; it is just presented differently through the menu of services and the fact that you are discussing the benefits and not the process. Let's face it, your clients are continually asking questions and you are giving consulting advice on steroids. Here is your chance to monetise this advice that you would normally be giving for free.

Make sure you have some services on the menu that have not previously been mentioned to the client. For example, an accounting firm could be offering business advisory services as part of its Platinum Package or for the client to have their own personal 'client manager' as part of the gold package.

When you start talking packages to the clients you are selling a product and the concept of time goes out the window. You can show the client all your services and offer to bundle these services with the packages. You could include your monthly newsletter in the package (another good reason why you could charge for the monthly newsletter: to give it value). You could also include webinars or even an invitation to your business retreat boot camps... the list is endless. The clients will feel like they are really getting some value for their dollar with you. And the more services they take on, the higher the fence you are building around the client. And the higher the fence, the harder it is for the client to leave.

Imagine if you could offer your client a $50,000 turnkey marketing package and on line marketing system. Do you think they would stay? And let's think about the business owner that is looking for a new accountant. Which one do you think they will choose...the one with the $50,000 marketing package or the one that doesn't have the $50,000 marketing system to offer as part of their service package.

You could categorise your client base and prepare different menu packages for each category. For instance you may have a business owner package specific to the needs and wants of business owners. You may have a package for investors. The business owner may be interested in some things in the investor package as they are looking at investing some money. And because you have indicated through your menu of services that you can help them with this, where do you think they will be going for this service?

You will need to prepare questionnaires for the clients to ensure that you gather all information pertaining to their needs, wants and expectations. The questionnaire will ensure that the client is made aware of every service that is applicable to them and that is also available to them.

You should prepare scripts for your menu of services to ensure that all the benefits are delivered properly. You could also prepare scripts for the meetings with the clients that will emphasise the benefits of fixed pricing.

You need to prepare a training program for the meetings to ensure that all team members are well versed on the benefits. This means that there will be a better chance of conversion and also a better chance of your clients wanting to buy more services from your firm (for their benefits of course). It also means that the work load for this project can be spread amongst the team members.

The next thing to do is set up a time for meeting with the clients. As an alternative, you can throw a party for your clients and announce the new exciting way of doing business. To get the best value out of this investment you must make sure you have a very good presentation about the benefits.

When we are talking to the clients about the benefits to them, we also need to tell them the benefits for us. We can tell the client that this will save us administration time and it means that we don't have to spend time chasing money owed to us. We can also focus on productivity and effectiveness when we don't have to account for time.

Have the meetings with the clients. Prepare a spreadsheet to keep a record of comments made in the meeting and also to measure the rate of conversion of clients that go with fixed pricing.

To summarise the step-by-step process:

- Prepare a menu of services.
- Prepare service packages.
- Categorise clients and prepare packages for each category.
- Prepare questionnaires for the meetings with the clients.
- Prepare scripts.
- Conduct meetings with all clients to discuss their fixed price agreements.
- Keep a record of the client interviews and note the conversion rate and find out why some clients did not convert.

TIP: The easiest way to find out what the client wants is to simply ask them. The clients won't know what you have to offer if you don't tell them via your menu of services. Imagine a restaurant without a menu.

HOW IT WORKS

The step-by-step process showed what needs to be done. It is important to have the process in place. It is just as important to have a strategy to make sure it works.

When you meet with the clients you use the questionnaires to gather information on their requirements. Show them the menu of services and ask them if there are any services they want that are not included on the menu. Discuss the firm's new concept of fixed price agreements and how this can benefit them.

Go through the packages showing all the menu of services for each category. From the answers to the questionnaires you will be able to see what other services the clients are interested in and these may be in a different category menu. This is an opportunity to bundle these services with the existing service. You also have the opportunity to bundle such things as newsletters and group webinars into the service offering and into the fixed price agreement. When you have finalised the list of services that the client wants, you can then ask the client what they would be prepared to pay for the package of services over the next 12 months. Before you go into the meeting you will have a pretty good idea of the service requirements for the client and you will also have a pretty good idea of the value for the fixed price agreement. When you ask the client how much they would be happy to pay for that service, you are empowering the client to have a say about the fees they are prepared to pay for the next 12 months. Mention to them that their annual fee can be paid in convenient monthly instalments and ask them what they would like to pay monthly for all the services indicated in the package. If they come up with a figure larger than yours, don't jump up and cheer. You need to then go through the benefits again and confirm with them that they are happy with that monthly fee. They will generally come up with a higher number than their previous offer.

You see, the most price sensitive person in a discussion about fees is *you*. And you will be surprised how many times the client comes up with a number bigger than the one you had in mind. It is their perception of value of the services that you are now offering.

You see, it is all about the client's perception of value. When you show them the benefits of the services, they can then ascertain the value of those services to them.

If the client is the one dictating the price, do you think you will ever have an argument about fees with them? As long as you deliver the service you won't have an argument, especially if you under promise and over deliver. And if you don't deliver, you don't deserve to be paid.

Meeting with the client to explain the fixed pricing structure and how it works also gives you an opportunity to explain the 'change order.' Let me explain...

If a situation arose where a project was outside the scope of the works in the fixed price agreement, the requirements for the project would be discussed. A change order will be prepared, showing the price for that particular project, and this price would be approved by the client before any work commenced.

With new clients the conversation always starts with, 'This is the way we do business here,' and then you present the menu of service and go through the questionnaire to ascertain their needs, wants and expectations. This takes out all the guess work.

To summarise why it works:

- Meeting with the clients will give you the opportunity of introducing your new menu of services.

- The questionnaire will ensure that all wants and needs of the client are offered and catered for in the fixed price agreement.

- By including things like all phone calls, meetings and emails in the package for the menu of service, the client cannot relate to last year's fees when thinking about the price. Their attention will be drawn to the value of the benefits in the future.

- You can work out the scope of work for the fixed price agreement with the client at that meeting.

- You can work out the price for the fixed price agreement based on the client's perception of value.

- You will avoid any fee arguments with clients with a fixed price agreement as long as you perform the service to a high standard.

- Look for the opportunity to bundle the services to add more value to the deal.

TIP: If the client dictates the terms in relation to the pricing of the agreement they will never argue about the fee, after all they determined the price. As long as you produce the goods there will be no arguments.

WHY IT WORKS

And now I suppose you are wondering why the client would pay you more in annual fees with the transformation to fixed pricing?

You see, when you show your client the menu of services they will be made aware of all the services that your business has to offer. Your clients will make enquiries about the services you have on offer as long as you make the services interesting. And also make sure you emphasise the benefits to the client.

This is where you can offer them more services and you can do some bundling of the services. And at every service level, included in the price will be unlimited phone calls, meetings and emails. When you offer these additional services to be included in the fixed price agreement, you should also express the benefit to the client. That is, they can contact you any time and discuss their business without the clock ticking away in the background. Let's face it, how many times have you spoken to a client for 20 minutes on the phone and sent him/her a bill for the 20 minute conversation? You don't send a separate bill for this because you know the client will complain. So you hide it away in WIP and then when it comes to invoicing time, that phone conversation was well and truly in the past and you won't put it on the invoice because you know the client will complain anyway. And deep down, you don't think that it is the right thing to do so you don't charge for it. This is an opportunity to monetise these phone calls.

Besides that, you should be encouraging your clients to contact the office on a regular basis. Enquiries almost always result in additional work, which means more fees, which will result in more profit.

Does it now make sense that you would include all phone calls in your fixed price? Besides that, when the client sees that inclusion they now feel that they are actually getting some real value from their accounting investment and are prepared to pay more for the additional service as they will be deriving more profit because of the service.

Think about it. What happens when a client phones you to have a chat about their business? The call will generally result in more business for you. How many times have you found that a client has purchased a motor vehicle or property and has not consulted you about it because they wanted to save money? That's right; they were too scared to call because they were worried about the clock ticking over at your end. And how many times could they have saved themselves, and you, a bundle of time and money on a transaction had they phoned you first? And worse still, how many times did they get a service from somewhere else because they wanted to save money by not talking to you when in fact you could have provided this service?

So you include phone calls, emails and meetings into your fixed price agreement. The next question might then be, (from the glass half empty people), "What if the client is on the phone for an hour?" The answer to that is… "Don't let the client talk on the phone for an hour." You let them know on the phone that this matter seems important and needs to be discussed face to face so you arrange a meeting with them. And then I'm guessing that the next question might be "But what if they take up more time in the meeting and I don't get more work out of the meeting?" And my answer to that is, 'Read this chapter again because you obviously don't get it.'

Have a think about it. Almost every time you have a meeting with a client there is an opportunity for more work. You may well be thinking that you'll be making less out of your fixed price agreement by doing more work. If you are not converting meetings into more work then you need to have a serious look at the way you are conducting your meetings. Some outside assistance may be required here.

If you are doing work for the client that is outside the scope of works in the fixed price agreement, then you need to discuss that all important 'change order' with the client. If the client talks to you about doing something outside the scope of the fixed price agreement, then bring it to their attention. Let them know you need to prepare a change order for the project, along with a price proposal so the client can approve it before any work is commenced. Do you see how this works? That's right get the price out of the way before any expense is incurred. Better to have the discussion about price before the job begins than having an argument when the job is finished.

We call this transparency. When professional people are not transparent with their clients this results in arguments that you don't need to have about the value of work performed.

To summarise why it works:

- Be transparent with your clients about pricing.

- Get the price out of the way before commencing the job.

- Show your clients the benefits and they will see the value.

- Meetings are an opportunity to do more work with your client so why wouldn't you include these in your annual fee?

QUOTE: With fixed pricing you have to give something away in order to get something back.

THE BENEFITS

There are several advantages in having a fixed price agreement with all of your clients:

- You have the opportunity of discussing your menu of services with the client. There will be services in there that they are very likely not aware of and could see how these services could be of benefit to them.

- You have that conversation with the client about money before the work is performed, which means you don't spend hours on a job only to find that the client does not want to pay you, or, worse still, has not got the money to pay you. You are better to discuss fees up front when you have no costs rather than at the finish of the job when all the labour and material costs have been incurred.

- You know what your minimum fee will be with the client.

- Your client will be happy knowing that their fee is fixed instead of getting ugly surprises in the mail every 12 months.

- You can establish the annual fee and ask for a proportion to be paid up front.

- The client can pay by monthly instalments or make instalments in certain months to suit their budget and cash flow requirements.

- You don't have to account for work-in-progress, which means you save time and money.

- You don't have to chase money from debtors as your clients pay one month in advance for services. Saving you time and money.

- You don't have to worry about debtors as all clients pay on the same day of the month. Saving you time and money.

- You will save an equivalent of 20 percent of your total revenue by not accounting for time, i.e. billing on a time cost basis. Our 'cost of time recording' spreadsheet calculation has proven this time and time again.

- You will have happier team members. You will retain good team members and attract new team members. Professional people are knowledge workers and they take offence at being seen as a six minute increment.

There are a number of cloud-based software programs around that enable the download of bank account details directly into the program. This is a very efficient way to gather information from your clients. This software (more details in the case study in chapter nine) will save you and your clients time and money and you need to encourage your clients to use this type of software. View this as a great opportunity to put a fixed price agreement together for the client, including installation and set up of this new software. The opportunities with fixed pricing are endless.

TIP: Design your fixed price agreements around your clients' wants and needs and include all phone calls, emails and meetings. This will encourage your clients to contact you more often and they will be happier. You will be conducting your business on a pro-active (rather than reactive) basis...a far less stressful way for you to do business.

CASE STUDIES

We conducted a Client Engagement Review for a 12 partner accounting firm. There was some great feedback from this process, but the most alarming item that came out was that every one of the 20 attendees at the Client Engagement Review said that they would prefer to have a fixed price agreement with the firm and not to be invoiced on a time cost basis. The attendees also agreed that they would be prepared to pay up to 25 percent more in annual fees if they could have a fixed price agreement with the firm.

One attendee commented that she did not like getting surprises in the mail and was really pissed off (her words) with being charged $1.30 for photocopying when her fees are in excess of $80,000 per annum. This attendee said that she would prefer to have a fixed price contract and pay $100,000 per annum. She went on to say that easy monthly instalments would also be a bonus. In addition to this, she also indicated that if she was charged for photocopying and phone calls again she would seriously consider moving to another accounting firm, and preferably a firm that was prepared to offer a fixed price contract. She also mentioned something about filing the invoice where the sun doesn't shine.

When we delivered the Customer Engagement Review report to the partners of this accounting firm, there was one thing they wanted to prioritise, and that was to offer fixed price contracts to all the clients that wanted them. Not all partners were convinced so we arranged to have a meeting with all the partners of the firm to go through our 'Cost of Time Cost' exercise. At the meeting we projected the time cost calculator spreadsheet on to a big screen. I arranged for one of the partners to input the information into the lap top.

This accounting firm had more than 80 employees and a turnover of $15 million. I won't go into the details of all the answers to the time cost questionnaire. The result from this exercise convinced a large majority of the partners to transition the firm from time costing to fixed price contracts. By the way, from this exercise we determined the time cost system was costing $2,823,960 per annum, almost 19 percent of total revenue.

When this figure popped out at the end of the calculation the partners were amazed. We put the question of accuracy to the group and asked if there was anything on the spreadsheet calculation that should be adjusted. Some of the partners indicated that, if anything, some of the numbers should be increased. This would have resulted in a further increase in this cost calculated for them having a time-cost system.

The purpose of the exercise was to give some indication to the partners of the costs involved with running their time cost system. The decision was made to implement our process for transitioning to fixed price billing.

The first thing we did was to work on a new menu of services. The firm did have information brochures detailing the services they provided but this information was all about the process and I could just imagine that any client, or potential client, reading this information would be asleep before they got to any of the good bits. Yes, it was extremely boring. There was nothing on this brochure that created the 'want' factor.

So we put together a menu of services that had a bit of life to it. The menu of services now showed the benefits to the clients rather than the process involved in providing the services. There were four packages available, going from bronze through to platinum. And the platinum service included business advisory services and we used terms like 'partnering' with clients and 'boost' profits. There were also additional specialised services in addition to the packages that could be bundled into any of the packages.

The next step was to prepare a menu of services for each category of client. Included in the client base were a range of business owners and also some high net-worth individuals, so there were different menus that were relevant to each category.

We worked on a questionnaire for the client meetings that would provide information on the clients' needs, wants and expectations. In going through the questionnaire the partners were able to determine the services required and were able to put together the structure of the fixed price agreement. There were a number of items on the menu of services that the clients were not aware of, even though they were mentioned in their previous information brochure. Here was a great opportunity to up-sell these services.

We put together the listing of clients for the interviews. In order to measure the success rate of the process, we decided that each partner would conduct team meetings over the course of the week and we would reconvene and discuss the results from those meetings.

There were a few partners that did not want to transition to fixed pricing and unfortunately they did their best to sabotage the process. These partners came back with a report that indicated that only a small minority of their clients were interested in transitioning to fixed pricing. We asked them to provide specific details of the clients and the comments made during the meetings. In order to resolve this issue we offered to interview the clients for them, and with them present, so they could improve their conversion technique. The request was denied and it then became apparent that they had not used the questionnaires in the interviewing process and in fact in some cases did not even discuss the menu of services in introducing the proposition of fixed pricing with the clients.

It was agreed by the majority of partners that these rebels would take no further part in the interview process with the clients. With the permission of the partners, we conducted the interviews with these clients and used the questionnaire in those interviews. We converted every one of those clients to fixed pricing.

We decided to measure the conversion rates for each of the partners so that we could assist any partners that may be struggling with the process. We arranged for some additional training for these partners.

There were clients that had genuinely declined the offer to transfer to fixed price contracts and fortunately these clients represented a very small percentage of the total annual fees.

The interview process continued for two months. The partners were happy with the result. The top 20 percent of clients, based on annual fees, had all agreed to transition to fixed pricing. This represented just over 75 percent of their fee base. The average fee charged for this group of clients increased by more than 15 percent with the transition to fixed pricing.

The next item on the agenda was to decide what to do with the clients that did not want to come on board. The partners were adamant at this stage that they wanted all clients to be on fixed price contracts and that they would eventually phase out time sheets when the time was right, and the sooner the better. They certainly would not be using time sheets for invoicing or determining productivity, so I am guessing they just wanted to hang on to them as a security blanket in order to complete the process.

The partners made a decision to engage us to interview those clients that had indicated that they did not want a fixed price agreement. We prepared a listing of these clients along with fees derived from these clients in the previous 12 months. We determined that the fees generated from these clients were just under $1.8m, so it was worth one last shot to get them across the line. We were successful in converting 60 percent of these clients. With the remaining clients, we bundled them up and engaged the services of a business broker to sell the fees (more about this process in chapter nine).

The initial part of the process was completed in three months. The result was that there was an increase in annual fees of more than $2 million from the clients that agreed to proceed with fixed price agreements. There were 155 clients that did not want to transfer to fixed pricing. This client population represented a fee base of $700,000. This fee base was sold to another accounting firm that could better service their requirements.

The timesheets were phased out after nine months, and after 12 months the firm had fixed price contracts totalling in excess of $19 million. The bottom-line net profit increased by 24 percent due to the increase in productivity.

And look at this for a result. By the time that timesheets were thrown out the window, the firm was saving over 1,000 man hours per month. No more WIP reports or WIP discussions, no more monthly invoicing (280 hours per month alone). No more WIP write-offs (previously around six percent per annum of total fees). No more problems with negotiating invoices with disgruntled clients after the completion of the project, which meant no more invoice write-offs. No more time spent on debt collection. No more bad debts. All fees collected in advance and received on the same two days of each month. There was an increase in the average fee per client as a result of the new menu of services. Defection rate for clients leaving the firm down to a small fraction of the pre time cost days.

The clients were happy. The team were even happier; they were now working on productivity instead of working on their timesheets.

ACTION STEPS TO ASSIST WITH THE IMPLEMENTATION OF THESE STRATEGIES

- Determine the cost of doing business using a time cost system.

- Prepare a menu of service for each category of client.

- Remember to show the benefits (and not the process) in your menu of services.

- Think outside the square when preparing the menu of services.

- Prepare a questionnaire that will help ascertain your clients' wants and needs.

- Meet with every client to discuss the menu of services on offer and agree on a fixed price agreement for the next 12 months.

- Convert all clients on to fixed price agreements and seriously consider selling those clients that do not want to proceed with a fixed price agreement.

Recommended Resources

'How to Win Friends and Influence People' by Dale Carnegie

http://www.amazon.com/How-Friends-Influence-People-ebook/dp/B0044XUINS

'Pricing on Purpose' by Ron Baker

http://www.amazon.com/Pricing-Purpose-Creating-Capturing-ebook/dp/B008L03YVS/

"Cost of Time Cost Calculation Spreadsheet" by Peter Lawson

For more information visit our web site at
www.businessdevelopmentspecialists.com.au

The Cost of Time Cost Calculation Spreadsheet has also
been included on the VeraSage web site at
www.verasage.com

CHAPTER 6

Taking That Mystery Out of Your Client's Perception

Do you ask your clients about how they perceive the service they are receiving from your accounting practice?

Do you conduct surveys?

Here's some information that we have found from our research on surveys (refer to recommended resources at the conclusion of this chapter for details of those surveys):

- Surveys take too much time.
- Surveys result in vague answers with results that don't really add growth in a business.
- Lack of follow-up with surveys.
- No anonymity – customers feel that by providing their personal details this means that they have to 'be nice.'
- Most surveys include too many long winded questions, making the customer put it in the 'too hard' basket.
- Customers feel like they don't have time to fill out surveys.
- Surveys are generic, boring and most customers will feel like they are repeating themselves.

Other findings:

- Surveys are easy but they provide little results.
- Customers who fill out surveys only write what they think you want to hear.
- Bias.

More information on these survey results can be found in the recommended resources below.

The best way to get the real answers from your clients as to how they perceive your services is to conduct a Customer Engagement Review (CER).

A CER helps the accountant gather first hand feedback from clients by providing a forum for open communication. Many times what is uncovered is that customers perceive that the business is indifferent to their needs.

Issues of perceived indifference are always revealed in the CER process. A CER will help the accountant understand what the issues are and how they can be rectified.

Your clients are the ultimate judges of the quality of your services and the processes you use to deliver them. Listen to your clients intently. Involve them in service design and seek their opinions on what you can do to create more value for them.

The accountant should never assume that they know what is best for their clients and, in particular, what they want their clients to do for them.

Firms that conduct regular feedback forums with their clients (and prospective clients) have their hand on the pulse and are much better placed to design services that their clients will value. This activity is also a phenomenally valuable service to offer to your clients for their customers.

TIP: If you want to know what your customers are thinking, have someone ask them.

THE STEP-BY-STEP PROCESS

To ensure the success of your CER, you must have an outside person act as chairperson for the CER in order to ask the appropriate questions. This is a good opportunity for you to engage a local businessperson into the process. A person considered as a sphere of influence in your local community. The following steps should be taken:

> ➢ Determine exactly what you want to achieve from the CER.
> ➢ Select a venue separate from your office (neutral ground) and date for the CER to be conducted.
> ➢ Determine which clients would be best suited to invite to the CER.
> ➢ Determine which prospective clients would benefit from an invitation to the CER.
> ➢ Send out invitations to the list of invitees.
> ➢ Finalise the questions to be asked at the CER.
> ➢ Select one or all of the partners of the firm to address the opening of the CER for the purpose of introducing the facilitator to the group and to explain why you are conducting the CER.
> ➢ Organise all partners to be in attendance at the conclusion of the CER to thank the attendees for giving up their time and to provide them with some refreshments.

> Gather the information from the CER and arrange a meeting with all partners and managers, and the facilitator, to discuss the outcome of the CER.

> Prepare an action plan going forward to be implemented over the next six to nine months. You could call this a customer focused marketing plan.

> Arrange to meet personally with all attendees within two weeks of the CER so that you can present the report from the CER and inform the attendees of your response to the feedback and the actions that you will be taking over the next six to nine months in order to respond to that feedback. Also present a small gift to the attendee to show your appreciation for giving up their time to attend the CER.

How It Works

Just imagine one of your clients sitting down at a luncheon with several other business owners. The subject of accountants comes up. What will your client say about you and **your** business? Will it be positive? Will it be negative? Or worse yet, will they say nothing at all? Will your client, instead, be silent, listening carefully to what's being said while internally thinking about the comparisons between your accounting practice and the one that's being discussed?

Clients are bound to think about you and the service your firm provides. Even if they aren't talking about you to other business owners, they evaluate you every time you provide a service.

It comes down to the issue of perceived indifference - the little things that communicate to the client that they aren't as important to your business as they think they should be. One of these 'little things' is the prime cause of lost customers: indifference. They leave because they feel the practice and its partners are indifferent to their needs, and they aren't as important to the business as they think they should be.

This 'indifference' can show itself in a number of different ways. Whatever they are in your practice, you owe it to yourself to find out what they are and fix them now!

When you think about it, wouldn't it be better to get your clients talking to you directly about their concerns, frustrations, and desires rather than telling someone else? Of course, but the benefits don't just stop there. Every day you wait, you risk losing a customer who feels unheard or un-cared for.

The CER process will take no longer than two weeks from start to finish. The actual CER meeting takes no longer than two hours.

The only thing you have to do is to determine who to invite, send out invitations, arrange the venue and then conduct the review. You can appoint a champion in the office to arrange all of this. The only other thing you need to do is to turn up at the CER to introduce the facilitator and then to ensure you are there at the end of the CER to greet your attendees and offer them a beverage. You will be amazed at the feedback you will get from your clients in that first 15 minutes after the completion of the CER.

The duration of the CER itself should be no more than two hours. The facilitator will ask a series of questions to the attendees and will welcome open discussion on all these questions.

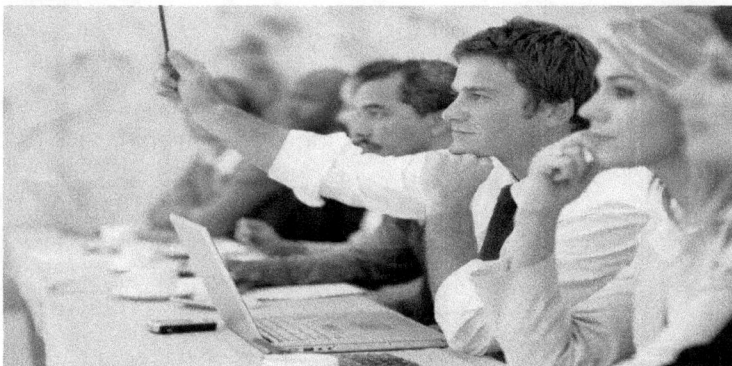

With the permission of all attendees, the CER will be recorded and the recording will be made available to the partners of the firm, again, with the permission of the attendees. The facilitator will have an assistant to ensure that he or she can focus on the facilitation of the meeting. It is also the responsibility of the facilitator to mention to the attendees that you will be preparing a generic report and that no specific names will be mentioned in relation to comments made in the meeting. This will ensure that the attendees have an open mind and will be totally upfront and honest with their responses to the questions that are put at the meeting.

Facilitation of a CER is not normally something for the faint hearted. The facilitator must be careful to ensure that all attendees have a say and that the meeting does not get out of hand when it comes to discussing some delicate issues. In the meeting, the only thing that the attendees have to do is to get involved and respond to the questions.

The final role of the facilitator is to meet with the partners of the firm subsequent to the CER and discuss the feedback from the clients.

To summarise how it works:

- Appoint an independent facilitator to run the CER.

- Determine invitees.

- Finalise questions for the group.

- The actual process will take less than two hours.

- Ask questions that will provide the answers you need.

TIP: When you ask the appropriate questions you will receive the appropriate answers.

WHY IT WORKS

Many times, what is uncovered in a CER is that clients perceive that the accounting firm is indifferent to their needs. Issues of perceived indifference are always revealed in the CER process. A CER will help the business owner, via a facilitation process, to understand what the issues are and how they can be rectified.

Your clients are the ultimate judges of the quality of your services and the processes you use to deliver them. Listen to your clients intently. Involve them in service design and seek their opinions on what you can do to create more value for them.

The accountant should never assume that they know what is best for their clients and, in particular, what they want their clients to do for them.

Accounting Firms that conduct regular feedback forums with their clients, and prospective clients, have their hand on the pulse and are much better placed to design services that their clients will value.

QUOTE: You won't get honest feedback like this from a survey.

THE BENEFITS

You will notice a change in posture with your clients after the CER. They will view you and the firm differently as they are now comfortable with the fact that if they have an issue with the service that they can bring this to your attention and you will listen and, even better, do something about it.

Your clients will be more open with you. They will tell their friends and colleagues about the CER, which means the word will spread about this unique process. It is very likely that some of the attendees will want you to do a CER for their business...more fees. And what do you think happens when you conduct a CER for your clients with 20 of their customers in the room? You guessed it; you have 20 potential clients in the room that may want to talk to you about doing a CER for them. They may also want to have a discussion about becoming one of your clients.

By ensuring that you visit all attendees at the CER within two weeks after the CER meeting, you have the opportunity to deliver the findings from the CER and to explain to your client the actions that your firm will be taking over the next six to nine months in order to address all the points raised. This is also a great opportunity to show your appreciation to the client by presenting them with a small gift. From our experience, you will always walk away with additional work from the post CER visitations.

In addition to that, the information you will gain from holding a CER is specific to your business, and represents a giant step on the path towards helping deliver the extraordinary service that will keep your clients coming back for more.

To summarise the benefits from conducting a CER:

- ✓ Adding value to clients by listening and responding to their needs.
- ✓ Obtaining feedback about your team and systems.
- ✓ Clients providing feedback on their need for additional services (some of which you may already provide but failed to communicate to your client), this leads to more added value work with the client.
- ✓ Gaining insights about what motivated people to come to the firm in the first place. This may assist the firm to discover its Unique Selling Proposition.
- ✓ You can get a real 'outside-looking in' perspective of your business.
- ✓ Help you identify what things you are doing well – so you can keep doing them.

- ✓ Give you ideas on what you can improve, and suggestions on how.
- ✓ Help you determine your priorities based on what your customers would like.
- ✓ Give your team a real sense of reward and focus so they're more motivated than ever before.

TIP: When you visit your attendees after the CER remember to take your order book. You'll need it.

CASE STUDIES

There are numerous case studies on the outcomes from the CER process. We conducted a CER for a second tier accounting firm and the main feedback coming from this was that the clients were not aware of all the services offered by the firm. The clients were not happy about being charged in six minute increments and were even more annoyed with being charged for things like photocopying and phone calls. We also learned that the attendees did not care whether compliance work was outsourced as long as it was supervised. The majority of attendees indicated that they would be prepared to pay more for a fixed fee rather than a time-based fee.

Then we conducted a CER with a manufacturer and importer. The participants at the CER mentioned that they were frustrated with some of the uniforms that were being supplied. Again, it was the little things that mattered, and in this case some of the shirts supplied by the business had tails on them that weren't long enough. This meant that every time the person wearing the shirt bent over, the tail of the shirt would pop out...not a good look. When our client addressed this issue, they not only increased orders with existing customers, but they were referred by their customers to several other customers. In addition to this, when our client visited the attendees at the CER, there was one attendee that had been made aware, at the CER, about a particular uniform that our client supplied. When our client visited this customer they placed a large order for that particular uniform.

At a small to medium sized legal firm the CER participants were very happy with the level of service provided to them but did not realise the firm was looking for more business. The attendees stated that every time they contacted one of the partners to offer a referral, the partner would explain how busy they were so the clients did not offer it as they did not want to burden the partners with any more work. When the partners of the firm visited the CER participants, to deliver a gift and thank them for their participation, they received more than 15 referrals to new business. In addition to this, the participants were not aware of all the services offered by the firm. The new menu of services resolved this issue.

This final case study will make you realize how the little things do in fact count. We conducted a CER for a mid-size financial planning business. The three owners of this business were very proud that they had acquired their own premises. The attendees thought that this was all well and good, but could never get a parking spot there as the partners occupied all the spaces. This meant the clients had to park some distance away and cart their files to the meetings. The attendees indicated that this was something that they did not like about dealing with this particular business. We presented this to the owners of the business and the cars were removed immediately from the parking area. When they visited their clients to thank them for attending the CER, they were very quick to note that there was now plenty of parking available at the premises and further, should they have any issues with parking, to let them know and they would arrange to have someone from the office park their car for them. These business owners had a great response from the post CER visitations, picking up a bundle of new work and referrals.

ACTION STEPS TO ASSIST WITH THE IMPLEMENTATION OF THESE STRATEGIES

- Arrange for a CER with your clients.

- Determine who will facilitate the CER.

- Consider offering the CER is a service that your firm could provide to your clients. Gather more information on how to carry out this process.

- Set a date for your CER.

RECOMMENDED RESOURCES

For a report on customer surveys refer to http://teamhively.com/433-customer-satisfaction-surveys-are-no-longer-relevant-pt1

More information on surveys at www.webpronews.com/customer-surveys-do-they-really-work-2007-09

To find out more about the CER process visit our web site at www.businessdevelopmentspecialists.com.au

CHAPTER 7

Outsourcing Your Compliance Work

Accountants, by their own admission, do not make good managers. They are technically good at what they do but they are not that good at managing their own practice.

It's crazy you know. Every time I visit an accounting practice the principal/ partners are always stressed and are pressed for time. They are working long hours, and unfortunately most of them are performing tasks that could be done by a university graduate. They just can't seem to get their hands off the tools and they are continually up to their eyeballs in work, most of it on a reactive basis.

The traditional accounting firm is filled to the brim with work. They always have more work than their team can feasibly handle, which means that the team members are continually overwhelmed. I can never understand why accountants wait until they are bursting at the seams before they even consider adding another staff member to handle the load.

When I question accountants about this situation the answer is in most cases that they just can't attract and keep good staff. And you wonder why when you look at the conditions they have to work under.

Accountants need to consider operating their practice more like a business than a practice. A business is run by managers who can manage. An efficient business works on repetition and efficiency. When you do something often enough you will do it well and with laser-like precision. Accountants try to be all things to all people and that's why they spread themselves so thin.

There is a solution to this problem and something that the accountant could seriously consider is to outsource all compliance work to a reliable bookkeeping service…and I do emphasise *reliable*. There are reliable bookkeeping services available. A good bookkeeping service is like a right arm to an accounting practice.

THE STRATEGY

In order to cope with the ever-increasing demand from clients, accountants need to free up valuable time to meet that demand. And the best way to do that is to outsource compliance work to a reliable bookkeeping service.

I understand that accounting firms have had some unsatisfactory experiences with outsourcing their compliance work and the main issues have been:-

- The work they receive back is inaccurate.
- Because the work received is inaccurate, the accountant has to correct the anomalies themselves as the job is running behind schedule.
- The work is not completed by the agreed date.
- The clients are concerned about their data being sent to an overseas entity.
- There were no checklists to ensure accuracy.
- The service is continually unreliable.
- Communication issues – language barriers.
- Lack of control with the process.
- Information misplaced.
- The service does not return phone calls.
- There are no regular progress reports on the jobs.
- The bookkeeping staff are asking all the wrong questions.

You can make outsourcing work. And the only way to make it work is to set out the rules of engagement. Make a list of everything you want the bookkeeping service to do, like a job description, and then interview the bookkeeping services to ensure that they are capable of performing the tasks that you want performed. You need to make up some checklists in order to ensure that the work is performed according to the agreed standards. You need to set performance standards.

The next item to determine is the nature of the work that will be outsourced. Will it just be bookkeeping work or will it be extended to other compliance issues such as completion of ASIC requirements, completed financial statements and possibly even preparation of income tax returns. I would take it as a given that the bookkeeping service will prepare the Business Activity Statements as part of their service.

For outsourcing to work you need to set down the rules and you need to ensure that the outsource service sticks to these rules. Always look for a bookkeeping service that will guarantee the quality of their work and also guarantee the date of completion. Look for the bookkeeping service that is prepared to put their money where their mouth is by offering a low risk, or even better, a no risk trial on say two or three jobs. And that offer could be something along the lines of…'Give us two jobs to complete and if they are not prepared according to your standards, and they are not prepared by the agreed time and date, then you don't have to pay for them.' And that would be good enough for me to give them the opportunity to prove themselves.

It is up to the accountant to make sure that the date set for completion will allow time for any adjustments that need to be completed by the bookkeeping service. In a real world, there will have to be some minor adjustments so the accountant has to also be realistic to allow some time for this. If there is not some time allowed for adjustments, the accountant will fall into that bad habit of doing those adjustments himself and then the system falls apart.

It is just as important for the accounting firm to have a process for outsourcing compliance work as it is for the outsource service to have a procedure for accurate completion of the work and having it completed on time.

TIP: Prepare a checklist of requirements before interviewing prospective bookkeepers for outsourcing.

THE STEP-BY-STEP PROCESS

When the decision has been made to outsource compliance work, the next thing to do is to put a procedure together to make sure it works. It is important that you involve the team in the entire process and seek their opinion on the extent of the work to be outsourced. Determine the performance standards for the outsource service. Prepare a list of expectations to ensure that the outsource service can meet these expectations and deliver the service in accordance with your performance standards. That way we are all on the same page.

Prepare a procedure to ensure that all information has been gathered from the client before delivery to the outsource service. An efficient outsource service will not accept delivery of a job unless all the information has been provided. And that will protect their deadline guarantee. One other thing to do is ensure that the bookkeeping service has the appropriate software to do the work.

Prepare checklists to ensure that all information is gathered from the client for delivery to the outsource service. I would not recommend using a bookkeeping service that did not have cloud based software to complete the work. This is another good reason for the accounting firm to transition their clients to cloud based accounting systems.

Prepare a comprehensive questionnaire for the interview process to ensure that the bookkeeping service can perform the work. The questionnaire could also ask whether the bookkeeping service offers a risk free trial.

HOW IT WORKS

There are a number of very reliable bookkeeping services that can perform compliance work more efficiently than an accounting practice.

I emphasise the word reliable here. The reliable bookkeeping service is run like a well-oiled machine. These businesses have systems and processes, just like any efficient business, and they are run by managers, who do not do any bookkeeping themselves. All they do is focus on managing the business and ensure that the business meets all the requirements of its clients.

These bookkeeping businesses have checklists for everything. They even provide checklists to the accountant to ensure that every piece of information (in order to complete the job) has been received. They will not accept a job until all the information has been received. And this is something that accountants should be doing with their clients as well.

Bookkeeping businesses do not have the distractions that accounting firms have. They do not try to be all things to all people, they just focus on one thing…getting the job done in an accurate and timely manner. The reliable bookkeeping business works on repetition. Just like the production line in a factory. They are not distracted by issues such as income tax, advisory services or financial planning services. All they have to do is follow their procedures, complete their checklists and pump out the work.

When the decision has been made to outsource the compliance work, and a satisfactory outsource service has been selected, now comes the time to make it all work.

All compliance work that is currently being performed in the accounting practice must be outsourced. Write a procedure for the transitioning of this work. Outsourcing every job is the best way to make this work. Compliance now becomes a production process.

The practice is now doing things differently and there should be a process in place that gathers the information from the clients and then passes it on to the outsource service. Checklists to ensure all the information has been gathered from the client. There should also be a process for checking the accuracy of the work being performed by the outsource service and also a process to ensure that the work is being performed on time. Make sure the bookkeeping service provides daily reports on the progress of the jobs.

Now there is the question regarding the accuracy of the work performed. And the best way to check accuracy is to reconcile it back to something and that something is a cash flow forecast. The accountant must prepare a cash flow forecast with their client. It is imperative that accountants sit down with their clients and prepare a cash flow forecast for a number of reasons, and particularly for the purpose of outsourcing.

Believe it or not, small business owners would like a 12 month roadmap that they can follow in order to reach their desired profit. Well the cash flow forecast is that roadmap.

I like to call it a profit forecast as this has more 'want' attached to it than 'need.'

In preparing the cash flow forecast the accountant can work through the expenses with the client. Expenses are the best place to start. They are regular and predictable. After you have worked out the monthly expenses you then ask the client how much profit they would like to make for the next 12 month. The only thing to discuss from there is revenue. The revenue is the variable part of the equation and can then be considered the target for the business in order to achieve the desired profit.

This opens up the door for the accountant to have deep and meaningful discussions with their clients on a monthly basis. The clients want this type of service and are prepared to pay for it. This is much better information for the client than hearing about how the financials were put together. And this service is perceived as real value by the client. Now they are getting some return for their accounting dollar investment. Can you see how something like this could improve client retention?

The best way to check the accuracy of outsourcing is by checking the monthly figures back to the cash flow forecast. The accuracy of the cash flow forecast is important. You must ensure that your accounting software can produce a monthly variation report. And how much could you charge for these meaningful monthly meetings? Better still, what are the odds of getting more work from the client out of these monthly meetings?

When the outsourcing entity indicates to the accounting firm that the monthly processing has been completed, the accountant can the run his/her experienced eye over the variation report. This is where the skills of the accountant come into play. They have the ability to look at the variation report and very quickly detect any material variances. The next step is to point these variances out to the bookkeeper (outsource service) so that they can check the entries to that expense account. If the entries are ok then the accountant should have a meeting with the client to discuss this material variation from the expense item on cash flow forecast.

This is a fantastic opportunity for the accountant to communicate with their client and to discuss doing more work with them.

For example, if there was a variation in advertising expense. The accountant could sit down with the client and ask the following questions:-

> Did you realise that you spent this amount of money on advertising for the month?

> The money you have spent on advertising is much higher that what we had originally budgeted for this month. Were you aware of that?

> When you arranged for this advertising did you ensure that you included something in the advertisement that will allow you to determine the return on your advertising investment?

> Would you like us to monitor your advertising expenditure on a monthly basis?

> Are there any other expenses that you would like us to monitor?

> When is a convenient time to arrange a meeting to discuss the measurement of the key performance indicators that have the most impact on your profit?

> Could we consider updating your cash flow forecast?

And because the compliance work has been outsourced, the accountant now has the time to have these meaningful discussions with the client. The accountant is now doing what an accountant should be doing instead of doing what should be outsourced to a reliable bookkeeping service.

SOMETHING TO CONSIDER: If an accountant is doing something that a bookkeeper could be doing, then the accountant can only be expected to be charging what a bookkeeper would be charging for performing that task…think about it.

WHY IT WORKS

There is an old saying…'horses for courses.'

Accountants have a range of skills to help their clients grow their business. When the compliance work is outsourced the accounting firm can free up an enormous amount of time. And that time can now be spent utilising all their skills and experience to help clients to grow their business. From my observations, most accountants use less than 30% of their available skills.

Small business owners need more from their accountant than just preparing financials and filling out some boxes on an income tax return. The accountant is the trusted advisor, and small business owners are looking more and more to their accountant to help them grow their business. And if their accountant does not have the time to provide this service, then they will find another accountant that does. Hence the importance of outsourcing the compliance work. The accountant must free up more time to spend with clients on growing their business and improving their bottom line.

When I look at the web sites for accounting firms they all look the same to me. They all say the same things, you know:-

> Our well trained staff will look after you.
> We have a professional team.
> We will minimise your tax legally.
> We are ethical.
> Our diligent staff will ensure confidentiality of your important data.
> We cater for all business types.
> We are reliable.
> We ensure that your work is accurate
> We have been around since 1922.

We call these platitudes.

And then the accountant wonders why it is that when a prospective client makes an enquiry, the first question they ask is the price. You see how price becomes the default question; it is the only thing they see as differentiating one accounting firm from another.

Accounting firms need to differentiate themselves from other accounting firms by including services and products that other accounting firms don't offer. They need to demonstrate the benefits and not the processes. The accounting firm that is prepared to show the benefits and why they are different will dominate their market.

Accounting firms do not have time to offer advisory services if they are doing compliance work. The accounting firm that handles compliance work is more often than not a reactive firm as opposed to being a proactive firm. The reactive firm is continually putting out fires. They are reactive to enquiries from clients about when their work will be finished; they are reacting to their client's cash flow problems, lodgement deadlines, and the list goes on.

By the time they put out all the fires, the accountant is exhausted and has no time left to address the real issues facing their clients…how to grow their business.

Accountants need to communicate more with their clients. Clients want more than just a meeting once a year to sign some tax returns and look at their very historic financials. Those days are gone.

Small business owners want more from their accountants and accountants need to work in a more proactive way with their clients. Proactive accountants are on the front foot. They address the issues before they become urgent issues. They don't have stressed out clients continually contacting them and asking them to put out fires, thereby causing a reactive response. Proactive accountants have the game in hand. They are communicating with their clients and working with them to help them with their business. They are available to answer questions because they are not bogged down with compliance matters. They return phone calls and enquiries in a timely manner. All of these actions will go a long way towards reducing client defection. The majority of clients change accountants because they perceive that the service they are receiving is indifferent to the service they expect.

THE BENEFITS

Imagine how much time can be saved by outsourcing compliance work. And this is a great opportunity to discuss fixed price contracts with your clients. A good bookkeeping service will be able to offer a fixed price for each job that the accountant refers. This makes the job easy for the accountant at the other end. They don't have to worry about what they will charge for the compliance work. All they have to do is approach their client and ensure that they are happy with the price before they proceed with the work. The outsourced compliance work can be bundled into the service package. The cost of compliance is no longer a variable.

There will be less pressure on team members. Their job will be to supervise the work that has been outsourced and to check the accuracy using the monthly variation statement. In other words, using their accounting skills to check the accuracy of the work presented instead of physically doing the work themselves. Accountants are knowledge workers and they are trained to do more than just prepare financials day in, day out. And the accountant wonders why they can't attract, let alone retain, good people.

The outsourced bookkeeping service will do all the heavy lifting for the accounting firm. The accountant's job will now be to communicate with the client and talk about the numbers. The accountant now has the time to explain what the numbers mean. They can also have a discussion with the client on how they can work together to improve those numbers.

To make all this work, the accountant will have to put some processes in place in the firm. The productivity in the accounting practice will improve. The accountant can learn a lot about processes and systems from a good bookkeeping service, especially in the area of gathering information from clients.

ACTION STEPS

1. Put a plan together for the transitioning of your compliance work to a reliable bookkeeping service.

2. Create procedures for the outsourcing of compliance work.

3. Construct a questionnaire for outsourced bookkeeping services.

4. Interview prospective bookkeeping services using your questionnaire.

5. Put a plan together for the time you will be freeing up in the practice after all the compliance work has been outsourced.

6. Look at some advisory service packages that will provide the tools to offer advisory services to your clients.

7. Think outside the square when it comes to advisory services and consider assisting your clients with marketing.

RECOMMENDED RESOURCES

Visit my website for an example to the tools available for advisory services:

www.newbusinessbreakthroughs.com.au

CHAPTER 8

8 – Eliminating Fee Disputes With Your Clients

I would love to have a dollar for every $10,000 left on the table of every accountant that did not adopt value pricing in their proposal and negotiation process. After several attempts I managed to master the art of value pricing with my clients and the skill is invaluable. I have learnt a lot from Ron Baker and Alan Weiss regarding the theory around this topic. I strongly recommend that you have a read of their books. Details are posted in the recommended resources at the conclusion of this chapter. Buy a big box of tissues before you start reading these books. You will be crying for days when you find out how much money you have been leaving on the table.

THE STRATEGY

Every accounting firm has to seriously consider the benefits of value pricing with *all* clients. The partners should have nothing to do with this process. They may be technically good at what they do, but they are really hopeless when it comes to pricing a job…way too price sensitive.

The major problem that accountants face with pricing a job is that they always look at the costs associated with the project, work those out, and then add on a margin for their profit. This is cost based pricing and it will never represent the value that an accountant is providing to his/her client.

The biggest problem with most accountants is that they undervalue themselves. This means that they don't expect anybody else to value the service that they provide. And that is the attitude they take into the negotiation ring when it comes to pricing a job.

If you are going to get serious about making some proper money out of your accounting practice you need to adopt value pricing. It may not be applicable to every project but there are some great opportunities that cross your desk and you need to be aware of those opportunities so that you can apply value pricing.

A good strategy is to consider engaging the services of a person that has expertise with value pricing. Yes, they are out there. These are people that do value pricing all day and they are very good at it. In the summarised organisation chart below, you will notice that I have a separate division for the "Value Council." You would have a director responsible for value pricing, assisted by a negotiation manager, and the administration for this would be outsourced. In a small accounting firm the director of value pricing and the negotiation manager will be the same person, or you may even consider outsourcing this to a contractible value pricing expert. Either way, what I am trying to get to here is that the professional and technical people in a practice should separate themselves from the pricing process. The only involvement that they should have with this process is to provide details to the value pricing expert. It will be up to the accountant to interview the client and determine the scope of works required to successfully complete the project. The valuation expert can then determine a price for the project (using the scope of works) and based on the *value* of the project to the client, not the *cost* of completing the project. The value has nothing to do with the costs that are to be incurred on the project. That is what I consider to be pricing backwards.

After the accountant has that initial meeting with the client, there will be a draft fixed price agreement prepared detailing all the benefits to the client along with the defined scope of works. This meeting will confirm that all items are covered in the scope of works. From there the client meets with the value pricing director to explain the value of the work to them and to discuss the price (in accordance with the value) of the project.

If you adopt value pricing, you will never have to enter into a conversation with a client about fees again. Fees are simply not something you deal with. Fees are discussed with the Value Council within the firm and are always discussed prior to the commencement of the project.

Now let's look at the situation without value pricing. Remember all the times when you received instructions from a client and completed the project to their satisfaction, but they were unhappy with your invoice afterwards and wanted to discuss it? Is that conversation a productive use of your time?

This all gets back to what was discussed in the earlier chapters. You have to be transparent with your clients or you are going to spend a lot of your valuable time explaining your invoices and negotiating part payment in of those invoices. The best thing to do is to separate yourself from the money and just do what you do best; leave price negotiation to someone who does it better than you.

When *you* are discussing a fee with a client, who do you think is the most price sensitive person in that conversation? If you said 'me,' you are correct. Let the client have their say on price after you have demonstrated all the benefits. I can tell you now, the price they have in mind is a lot higher than the one you have in mind. And the price they have in mind in anticipation of the project being completed is higher than the price they have in mind after the project has been completed. So, do yourself a favour and leave pricing to the experts.

Have a look at the summarised organisation chart below to see where value pricing now fits into the professional organisation. Ron Baker calls this a Value Council,' in his book, 'Implementing Value Pricing.'

You will notice on the organisation chart that the administration work is all outsourced.

SALES AND MARKETING	MANAGEMENT ACCOUNTING	TAXATION AND COMPLIANCE	HUMAN RESOURCES	VALUE COUNCIL
Director of sales and marketing	Director of management accounting	Director of taxation and compliance	Director of human resources	Director of value pricing
Manager of sales and marketing	Manager of management accounting	Manager of taxation and compliance	Payroll manager Training manager	Negotiation manager
Outsourcing service	Outsourcing service	Outsource service	Outsource service	Outsource service

(Organisational chart headed by BOARD OF DIRECTORS and CHIEF EXECUTIVE OFFICER)

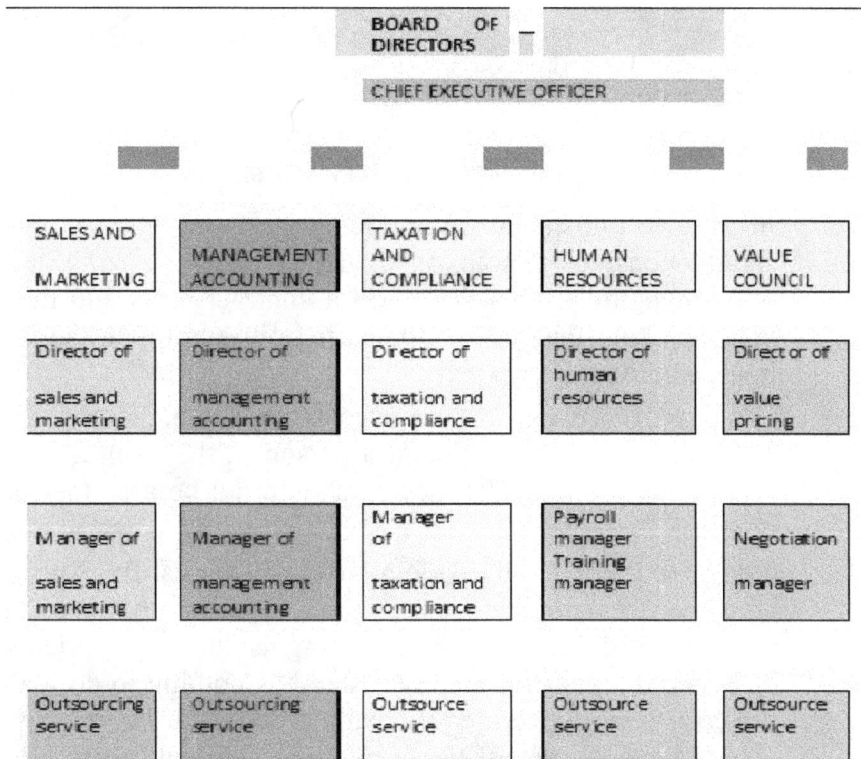

To summarise the strategy:

- Always look at the value of a job to the client when pricing, as opposed to the costs incurred in completing the job.

- Engage the services of a value pricing expert to assist with the pricing for your fixed price agreements.

- Separate yourself from the money.

- Be transparent with your clients about price and save yourself a whole heap of time.

- Discuss the benefits - not the process.

THE STEP-BY-STEP PROCESS

In order to implement value pricing into your practice, you should consider appointing a value pricing expert. Start with engaging their services on a contract basis and then you may find that you can benefit from employing an in-house value pricing expert.

For those that want to have a go at this on their own, the best thing to do is to appoint a person in the firm to look after value pricing. That person should not be a partner of the firm.

You should apply value pricing to every annual fixed price agreement, every change order and any project that you do. As the word implies, value pricing is all about pricing based on the value to the client and has nothing to do with the cost to complete the job or the process. Of course, you should have an idea of the costs associated with the job to verify that your value price is sufficient to cover those costs.

Let's take for example your fixed price agreements that have to be renewed annually. Arrange to meet with the client to discuss their requirements for the next year. A questionnaire will be handy to identify the client's needs and wants and to discuss anything you can improve on in order to improve the service.

When you have allowed the client to select the services that they need and want for their business, you need to then start talking to the clients about the benefits. Let the client tell you how they will be benefiting from each of the services and then ask the client how much the benefits of those services are worth to them. That's right; let them come up with a number. I can assure you it will be higher than the number you had in mind. And when they come up with that larger number, don't pull out the champagne and celebrate, you should go over the benefits again and allow the client to re-assess the value of those benefits, and, on almost every occasion, they will come up with a higher value again.

Can you see how you are allowing your client to dictate their own terms when it comes to money? They are assessing the value and the benefit of the services your firm provides.

If the client is telling you what they think they should pay, then provided you deliver the service, do you think they are ever going to complain about their accounting fees? Have a think about all the time you will save by being transparent and getting the money out of the way before you start the project. And also have a think about how much money you have left on the table, just in the last 12 months. And think about the time that can be saved by having someone other than a partner involved in the value pricing process.

You may also have a situation where a client's perception of the value is way below your expectations. If you can't get that client to realise the value that you will be providing, then it is a good time to let that client move on, or even consider the client for the clearance bin (referred to in chapter nine).

TIP: Allow the client to dictate terms on what they want to pay. They will often have a higher price in mind than you. Allow the client to express their perception of the value they are receiving.

How It Works

How would it work if your clients determined the fees they paid on each project? If you let your clients determine the amount of fees they are happy to pay on each project do you think they would ever complain about their fees?

Provided that you produce the goods on each project and you perform all the tasks as agreed by the client, there is no reason for the client to complain about fees.

Value pricing will bring your client's attention to the value and take them away from thinking about the cost or the price for the project. They can make an informed decision based on the benefits they will receive from the project and they can calculate the return on their investment in accounting services.

I have had some Neuro-Linguistic Programming (NLP) training and I highly recommend that any professional, dealing with people, complete an NLP course. This would be particularly helpful for value pricing discussions and negotiation for fees.

NLP will assist you in dealing with your clients either in pricing negotiations or assisting them in general.

I am not going to go into any more detail here about NLP and I will leave some details in the recommended resources so that you can follow this up for yourself.

TIP: Have a look at the courses available on how to deal with people and how to gain their rapport. When you know how to gain rapport the rest of the game is easy.

WHY IT WORKS

Why is it that accountants do all the work on a project and pay all the costs associated with the project, only to find at the end of the project that the client is not happy with the fee and wants to argue about it? Who do you think is in the better position to argue?

The accountant is sitting there looking at the costs incurred and thinking about their recovery instead of the benefits the client has received from the project.

Wouldn't it be easier to discuss the fee for a project before the project starts and before any costs are incurred?

Let's look at an example to give you some clarity on this. And remember, this is an exaggerated example to give you an idea on how the value pricing process works. I am in no way suggesting that any doctor would ever do this with a patient.

There you are one day, just going through the motions and all of a sudden you have this excruciating pain in your left side. You can't move and an ambulance comes to the office and carts you off to hospital. You go straight into the emergency ward and the doctor asks you some diagnostic questions and then informs you that you have a burst appendix and if you are not operated on within 24 hours it could have very serious consequences and very likely lead to death. The doctor then asks you what you would like to do. Before you answer that question, bear in mind you are still in a bus load of pain.

In this situation I am sure you would ask the doctor to remove the appendix, which of course will remove the pain, which means that there is a better than even chance that you won't die.

The longer you leave your decision, the more likely the situation could be fatal.

So the doctor brings in the surgeon. And the surgeon asks you if you would like him to perform the operation within the next hour. You are in so much pain. The longer you wait for the operation the more chance you have of dying. What do you think you would say to the surgeon?

I'm sure you would be pleading with the surgeon to remove that stinking appendix, along with the pain, and as soon as possible. So, at this point, does the surgeon explain the procedure for the operation? Does he tell you how he has to be very careful how he makes his incision and how he is going to remove the appendix? Is he also going to explain all the costs associated with doing that? I don't think so. And, because you are in so much pain, would you listen anyway?

The surgeon doesn't explain the process. Instead he or she talks about the benefits of having the appendix removed; you will no longer be in excruciating pain and there is less chance of you dying. I would think that right at this point of time, these are pretty good benefits. The surgeon is your saviour. So, when the surgeon asks you to confirm you want to proceed immediately with the operation you reply by saying, "Yes please, I would really appreciate that". The surgeon then discusses the fee.

The point I am making here is that the fee is discussed up front by the surgeon, based on the result. The surgeon has ascertained your needs and wants and has clearly set out the benefits from proceeding with the operation. And you would really like to get things started.

There was no argument about the fees or paying the fees prior to the operation as the benefits were discussed and agreed upon. The surgeon could have allowed you to have your say about the value of the operation to you, i.e. the value of the operation to you given the benefits that you will be receiving and the fact that the operation will be over and done with in less than an hour. All you are thinking about is that in less than one hour, you will have no pain and you are not going to die.

If you were asked how much you would like to pay for the operation, how much would that be? Would it be $10,000 or maybe even $20,000? What would you have done with the money if you were not alive to spend it? I don't know about you, but I would have been prepared to pay $20,000 for this operation. It's all about return on investment.

The point I am making here is that the surgeon has literally left up to $10,000 on the table because he/she did not consider the concept of value pricing.

Let's look at this situation from another angle. You are still lying on the bed in hospital in bus loads of pain. The surgeon has explained the process (instead of the benefits) of not having the appendix removed as soon as possible.

You still agree to go ahead with the operation as soon as possible. But in this scenario the surgeon does not discuss the fee for the project up front. Instead the surgeon, with your consent, proceeds with the operation, successfully removes the appendix, stops the pain and prevents you from dying. So nothing else has changed from the previous situation. The outcome is exactly the same.

It is now three weeks after the operation. You have fully recovered and are feeling brand new. You are in no pain and you didn't die. You have an appointment with the surgeon...a procedural check-up so to speak. The surgeon asks you how you are feeling. And you respond, "Great, thanks to you."

The surgeon asks you some questions to ensure you are in good shape and then says, "Okay, you are good to go. There is just one thing to finalise before you go, and that is the payment of my fee. The fee for the operation is $10,000 and here is your invoice."

You look at the invoice and say, "This is ridiculous, I was in and out of the operation in less than one hour and you want to charge me $10,000 for that? I can't afford this, how much will you accept if I pay now?"

The surgeon then explains all the expenses that he/she incurred for the operation and you still don't get it. You still cannot see the value, and the reason for this is that you have already received the value and the operation is not as valuable now as it was when you were lying in pain in the hospital. The surgeon now faces a dilemma and looks at the expenses incurred and the other thing the surgeon is thinking is "How much do take off this bill so that I can finalise this matter and to get this unreasonable person out of my office?"

Does this second scenario sound familiar? How many times have you had a client absolutely pleading for your services? They may have a project that is a matter of life or death for them and be in a lot of (financial) pain. Like the nice person (not necessarily clever) person that you are, you go ahead and complete the project successfully without discussing the value perceived by the client or the fee the client is prepared to pay for the successful completion of the project.

In order to complete the project as quickly as possible you bring in other team members and, worse still, you take these team members away from the paying jobs they are currently working on.

You complete the project successfully and in record time, then sit down with the client and discuss the results. The client is so happy that you have not only saved him/her a bundle of money, you have prevented their business from going belly-up because of your brilliant negotiation skills.

At the end of the month you print out the work-in-progress report from your abacus, I mean time cost system, and this shows an amount of $12,000 for the project. You spend an hour going over the WIP report in detail to make sure nothing has been overcharged and you decide to take $2,000 off the bill and invoice the client for $10,000, thinking you are giving value or doing the right thing. A month goes by and the client has not paid the invoice. So you contact the client to ask why he/she has not paid and they start arguing about the fact the bill is too high and he/she cannot afford that kind of money. You then get the client in for a meeting to go through the invoice and to show him/her your time cost records that indicate you could have charged $12,000 for the project. At the meeting the client claims that the WIP report means nothing and says that you can put anything you like on a timesheet. In addition to that the client argues you are trying to charge $10,000 for three days work. What this all really means is that you have just wasted another two hours of your life with the client when you could have been at home cleaning fridge magnets...the productivity level would be much the same.

On the other hand, if you had the discussion about fees with the client before you started the project...when the client was in a great deal of pain, thinking he/she was going to lose his/her business, the house, the lot...I am sure the conversation would have been different. The client, being made fully aware of all the benefits they would derive from the completion of the project, would very likely have been prepared to pay three times that amount and a substantial proportion up front. But instead, here you are, you have spent money on this project, taken other team members away from paying projects, used all your skills and experience, (that took many years to perfect), worked your butt off to get a result, reduced the invoice to give the client an extra good deal, and this client then has the hide to refute your invoice and only after you made contact with them. The client is virtually calling you a thief by saying that you are overcharging. The client gets the better of you and you knock another $2,000 off the bill just to keep him/her happy.

This scenario is further proof of the problems with timesheets. Have a think about when you go to the dentist. The dentist has a look at your teeth and says you need a filling in a tooth. You say, "Okay let's do the filling." The dentist is very skilful and finishes the job in 15 minutes. He or she gives you a bill for $400 and you say, "Hang on, you only took 15 minutes to do that filling and you want to charge me $400?" The dentist then asks if you would like him/her to drill for another hour so you can get your money's worth. Do you get my drift? It's all about value, not the process or how long it takes. Reasonable people are even prepared to pay more for having the project completed quickly. Think about this concept and then think about how much money you have left on the table.

Remember, it's all about the return on investment. Allow the client to calculate the value of their benefit from dealing with you and then allow them to determine how much they are prepared to invest in accounting fees for the successful completion of the work. Does that make sense?

THE BENEFITS

The main benefit stemming from value pricing is that you are allowing the client to recognise the benefits they can gain from the project. When you apply value pricing you can allow the client to dictate some terms regarding their perceived value and what they are prepared to pay for the benefits.

Involving the client in the pricing process will ensure that you don't waste any time arguing about money with the client.

Value pricing is not about squeezing every last penny out of the client. It is about finding out the client's perception of value. It is all about you explaining the benefits to the client. The problem with accountants is that they undervalue themselves. And in particular, they don't value their ability as much as the client does. That is why it is a good move to appoint a person that is an expert at value pricing. They are not emotionally involved in the project and have the ability to make the client look at the value of the benefits they will derive from the completion of the project.

It is all based on the client's return on investment. When you explain the benefits, the client can then assess the value to them of receiving these benefits. At that point they can then determine how much they want to invest (in accounting fees) to derive that benefit.

By appointing another person to look after the pricing of projects you are separating yourself from the money and discussions with the client about money so you can just get on with the job of producing the best result for them.

Have a think about the number of hours you have spent discussing money with clients, whether it be discussing your fee up front or arguing about your fee at the end. Think about the opportunities that have passed you by while you were spending time talking about money. Discussing money is not your core business; stick to your knitting and generate profit for your clients. By assisting your clients with advisory services the fees you charge will become a very small percentage of the additional profit that the client will be deriving. So why would a reasonable client ever complain about fees when they are deriving a very attractive return on their investment in your services.

And have a think about how much money you have left on the table by not having the value pricing discussion with the client. That would probably pay for 10 value pricing experts.

To summarise the benefits:

- No more time spent having those pricing discussions with clients.

- No more lost opportunities from time wasted in dealing with pricing.

- No more arguments with clients about your fee after the event.
- Separate division that focuses on the pricing process.
- Less money left on the table which means more money to spend on team training.
- Direct the client's focus to return on investment for your services.

TIP: Separate yourself from the pricing process. Pricing should be a separate division within the firm.

CASE STUDIES

I worked with a legal firm to assist with value pricing some of their projects. We had a meeting with a client who was in a very serious predicament. The client was about to lose his business, he had some issues with the Australian Taxation Office (ATO), some issues with other creditors, and some issues with a debtor who did not want to pay a large invoice. These three issues would be enough to close down the company that he had successfully operated for over 20 years. He would have to sell the family home to cover his personal guarantees (he did not receive very good advice on asset protection) and the children would have to come out of their private schools. He would have to find a job, and it was looking very likely that both he and his wife would have to declare bankruptcy in order to sort the whole thing out.

I was engaged by this very progressive legal firm to assist with value pricing. They were in the process of moving on to fixed pricing throughout the entire firm. So when I mentioned value pricing in relation to the project above, they were all ears. In order to convince some of the partners that value pricing does work, we ran timesheets for the project to determine the price that would have been charged for the project on a time cost basis.

One of the partners in this firm was the insolvency expert and had a great rapport with the ATO and was able to negotiate with the appropriate people. So we knew we had the ATO side of the project well and truly covered.

The partners assessed the project and looked at it from the client's perspective, the pain they were going through, and the benefits they would derive from a successful outcome. The root of the problem was that the client's debtors were not paying on time. This was causing cash flow issues that meant the client was behind with ATO commitments and they had some other creditors that were running out of patience.

He had one particular (larger) debtor that he had problems with collecting the amount owed on his long-outstanding account. This issue had to be resolved.

The partners knew from their information gathering that they could hold off the ATO, and they could sort out the issue with debtors (by using a Cash Flow Control Program). In addition to that they could resolve the issue with the larger debtor who was refusing to pay. The partners communicated with this debtor and found that there were some very minor items of dispute with some invoices and he was not prepared to pay his account until these issues were resolved. The partners obtained an undertaking from the debtor that when these items are resolved that he would pay his outstanding account in full. As it turns out, this was just a communication glitch. The receipt of these funds would have a significant effect on the outcome.

The money coming in from the debtors (from the implementation of the Cash Flow Control Program) would resolve issues with the other creditors and would assist in negotiations with the ATO. In other words, we could hold off the wolves while getting the ship back in order and, hence, avoid the unpleasant situation of tipping over.

The partners involved in the project thought that $50,000 would be a good price for this project as they had a pretty good handle on the outcome. I asked them how they arrived at that and they started telling me about the time it would take and the costs involved and their profit margin. We then discussed having a meeting with the client and going over the benefits that he would derive from their experience. Let's have a look at the benefits:

- ✓ The client's company would not go into administration (and possibly liquidation)
- ✓ The client would keep the family home
- ✓ The client would no longer have to worry about the threats from the ATO
- ✓ The client would not have to pay hefty fees for the administration /liquidation process
- ✓ The cash flow problem in the business would be resolved
- ✓ The client's children could remain in private schools
- ✓ The client and his wife would not have to go bankrupt and carry that stigma with them for the rest of their lives
- ✓ The debtor refusing to pay the large invoice would be paying the outstanding amount, as per our negotiations, and this would resolve a fair chunk of the cash flow issues in the business
- ✓ The client would have less stress and be able to sleep at night
- ✓ The client would have more quality time with his family
- ✓ The client would not be living in fear of losing everything he had worked his butt off for over the last 20 years
- ✓ The client would not have to look for a job
- ✓ The client would have a clean slate with the ATO

✓ The client would have time to re-build the business with some planning

To cut a long story short we had a meeting with the client and took the time to understand his needs, wants and urgency to resolve his issues. We then went through the benefits that would be enjoyed from the successful outcome of the project. We made sure he understood the benefits and also the ramifications if we did not carry out this project for him. We then asked the client what all that was worth to him, i.e. the value of saving his business and all his personal assets that he had worked so hard to get. He came up with a value of $200,000. He also offered to pay half up front and another portion when we received the money from his large outstanding debtor. The remaining amount would be paid from the increase in cash flow generated by implementing the cash flow program.

My client, the legal firm, ran some timesheets in parallel with the project. They made sure that everyone in the firm recorded every minute of their time spent on this job, even the administration people.

The project was completed in less than three months and the client appreciated that the project was not drawn out.

The partners of the legal firm were delighted that their client valued their services for this project at $200,000. They could have left $150,000 on the table by not allowing him to value their services. Believe me, the return on investment for the client was huge.

The client was happy. The $200,000 represented a very small percentage of the value of the possible ramifications to him without the service. By the way, at the end of the project, when everything was back in order, the client admitted to one of the partners that he would have been prepared to pay more when they were initially discussed the project.

And you were wondering what was on the work in progress report at the end of the project? All they could notch up (with mark-ups) was $32,000.

I rest my case.

ACTION STEPS TO ASSIST WITH THE IMPLEMENTATION OF THESE STRATEGIES

- Write down the amount of money you have left on the table with traditional pricing

- Enquire about engaging the services of a value pricing professional

- Create a new division in the firm for value pricing all projects

- Implement value pricing

- Separate the technical people from the pricing process

"Value Based Fees - How to Charge and Get What You're Worth" - by Alan Weiss

http://www.amazon.com/Value-Based-Fees-Charge-Youre-ebook/dp/B006208UBY/

"The Consulting Bible - Everything You Need to Know to Create and Expand a Seven Figure Consulting Practice" - Alan Weiss

http://www.amazon.com/Consulting-Bible-Everything-Seven-Figure-Practice/dp/0470928085

"Implementing Value Pricing" - Ron Baker

http://www.amazon.com/Implementing-Value-Pricing-Business-Professional/dp/0470584610

"Neuro-Linguistic Programming" - Matt Catling at Kaliber Events. For more details visit their web site
www.kaliberevents.com.au

CHAPTER 9

9 – Less Clients = More Profit

Let's face it, when you start your own accounting practice you will take on anybody that fogs a mirror. You keep thinking that the more clients you have, the bigger you are. You might be bigger, but this doesn't mean you are all that profitable. And what invariably happens is that five years down the track you have all these (now unsuited) clients creating a whole heap of stress.

You have moved on but some of your clients have not really moved on with you and to do the right thing by those clients you need to move them on to another accounting firm that can better cater for their needs and wants.

This chapter will show you how to make more money, and spend less time doing so, and with less than half of your existing client base. The purge process can be a great tool for finding hidden profits in your accounting practice.

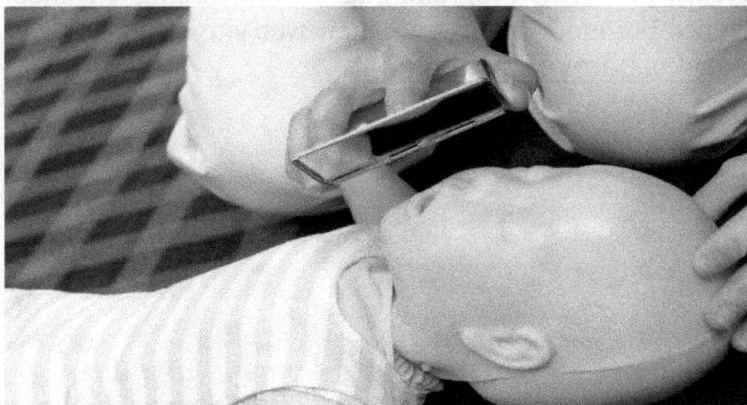

THE STRATEGY

You need to have a good look at your client base at least once every three years, preferably on an annual basis. I know of some financial advisers that continually cull the bottom 15 percent of their client base to make way for more valued clients.

As accountants we need to continually free up valuable time to spend more time with the clients that are willing to pay for the value you deliver to them. Accountants are funny. Let me explain...

The accountant accumulates a large client population. Each of these clients represents administration time. There are some good clients and some not so good clients. There are some clients that pay more fees than others. There are clients that pay very little in fees but still take up more than their fare share of administration time. There are clients that pay on time and there are clients that you have to continually chase for money. And there are some clients that just don't pay at all. There are clients that present their work on time and in a very efficient manner and there are clients that are continually putting pressure on your lodgement deadlines.

We could compare this to an aeroplane where you have the first class passengers in the front spending much more than the economy class passengers in the back. The front of the plane takes less time to look after yet they represent a higher percentage of the total fares on the plane.

The passengers in the front of the plane are waving $1,000 notes and saying help me, spend more time with me, I am prepared to pay for more of your services. Whereas, the passengers in the back of the plane are waving $5 notes and saying I want more of that great knowledge and experience but I am not prepared to pay more.

Have a good think about this. You have clients in the front line of your business that are great to deal with and want to spend more money with you, but you don't have the time to spend with them because you are attending to the clients at the back end of your business.

You need to free up valuable time to spend with the clients that value your expertise and are prepared to pay for it. They have already calculated their return on investment.

How do you find this time? The best way to do it is to purge the client base and apply the Pareto Principle to the client base to determine where the majority of the fees are coming from. The Pareto Principle (or 80/20 Principle) states that there is an inbuilt imbalance between causes of results, inputs and outputs, and effort and reward. A good benchmark for this imbalance is the 80/20 relationship: a typical pattern will show that 80 percent of the fees derived by an accounting firm will be from 20 percent of the number of clients. There are a number of books that detail the Pareto principle and these will be shown in the recommended resources at the conclusion of this chapter.

TIP: Purge your client base at least every three years.

THE STEP-BY-STEP PROCESS

The process for determining your most profitable clients is not rocket science. There are some systems around that will provide the information you need for this process.

The first thing to do is to prepare a list of the clients of the firm. This spreadsheet will list the clients from highest fees to lowest fees. Calculate the total fees from this listing. Then add the revenue from each client as you go down the list. Accumulate this total and when you have reached the amount that represents 80 percent of the total fees, draw a line under that client.

Go back to the list and calculate the total number of clients on the list above the line. You will very likely find that 20 percent of your total client base (in number) will be above the line representing 80 percent of fees.

The next step in the process is to sit down and prepare a clear definition of your 'ideal client.' I would strongly recommend that you approve the definition of the ideal client with your managers and team members. They may have something to add as they are on the front line of the firm.

An example of an ideal client could be put into point form as follows:

- ✓ Pleasant nature.
- ✓ Supplies information in a timely manner.
- ✓ Willing to listen to advice.
- ✓ Respects the advice they receive.
- ✓ Supplies accurate information.
- ✓ Can afford to pay their fees.
- ✓ Is prepared to refer clients to the firm.
- ✓ Wants more service than just compliance work.
- ✓ Does not continually complain about fees just for the sake of having an argument.
- ✓ Prepared to implement suggestions.
- ✓ Prepared to pay their fees on time.

This is a good list to start with.

From your client listing you need to have a look at the clients above the cut-off line and initially, you need to ensure that these clients are in fact 'ideal clients' in accordance with your checklist. For those clients that do not fit the definition there may be some things you can recommend so that they can. There is nothing you can do about a client that is not pleasant, they are first to go.

There will be some clients who provide you with sloppy information and/or don't supply the information in a timely manner when requested. If these clients are prepared to listen to some advice on changing the way they provide information, then you can overcome this problem. If not...consider them for the clearance sale.

You need to have a good look under the line as well and make sure there aren't any clients under that line that have potential for growth, have shown an interest in taking advantage of advisory services offered by the firm and/or are a great referral source.

This is a great opportunity to get rid of relatives from your client base. They can sometimes be an unnecessary evil. You have to be ruthless with this process. The correct way to think about this process is that these clients can be best served with another accounting firm and you are doing the wrong thing by the client in not giving them the opportunity to do so. You could also take the responsibility of selecting that accounting firm for them.

If your are thinking of transitioning your client base from time cost billing to fixed price contracts this is a perfect opportunity. You can interview all your clients that fit your 'ideal client' definition and introduce them to your new menu of services and determine their needs and wants. It's also a chance to let them know that this is the way you will be doing business from this point onwards. It is also a great opportunity to express the benefits for them in proceeding with a fixed price agreement.

The process for the transition to fixed price agreements is also a great opportunity to sell more services to your clients and hence derive more fees from them. It is an opportunity to gain more rapport with your client base and introduce your clients to a new cloud-based accounting system. If you are having problems gathering accurate information from your clients, or just gathering information, this is a good way of seeing whether they are prepared change the way they do things so that these problems can be overcome, which in turn will result in a more effective delivery of service. You could include the changeover to the new accounting system as part of their new fixed price contract...a double whammy.

On completion of the interviews with your clients you will know who's who in the zoo. You will know who is happy to listen to your recommendations for change and who is prepared to make these changes to benefit both parties.

This is just another part of the elimination process. After the elimination of clients from this process, you should again assess your fee base and apply the Pareto Rule to that data base. Draw the line. Those above the line will be retained. You should also look below for those clients that have potential for more growth, although most of these would have been identified during the interviewing process.

You may well ask why we would interview all the clients that come under the definition of ideal client. That question will be answered under the Why It Works heading of this chapter.

TIP: You must adopt an objective approach to culling your clients. The remaining clients must fit your definition of ideal client.

How It Works

E-Bay is a platform whereby people sell the things they no longer want to somebody who appreciates and benefits from those things. Put simply, "one man's trash is another man's treasure and beauty is in the eye of the beholder." Why hang on to something you no longer gain pleasure from? Why not pass that something over to someone else who can appreciate the item and make better use of it and you can also get some money for your trouble. By offloading the things you don't want you free up storage space. You are not tripping over the item and thinking when you are going to do something about it. You are also freeing up your head space.

Circumstances change. You move on and you improve. You grow your firm and you want to continue to grow your firm. Not all of your client base will move on and progress with you. It is human nature. Most of your clients were very small business (or even salaried employees) when you first took them on. Three years down the track, the size of your client base has doubled, you have grown, you have progressed and moved forward and you have a different client base. You have clients that want you to help them grow their business and improve their bottom line. They want to grow their business and they need your help. In fact, they need more of your time than you can currently afford to give them. And the reason why you do not have any time is that you are still servicing the clients that do not want to progress forward with you. The clients that do not want to take advantage of utilising all that you have to offer in knowledge and experience.

These clients still want your attention and you have an obligation to service their needs as long as they are a client of your firm. You know deep down that these clients would be better off being served by an accounting firm that can better cater for their needs and wants, and can give them the level of service that they want. Your practice is not positioned to provide that level of service any more. You have moved on. You need to do the right thing by you and your clients and find them an accounting firm that can better cater for their needs.

The application of the Pareto Rule will indicate your most valuable clients. It will tell you where a majority of your profit is coming from. When you have a good hard look at the list you will find that there is not much difference in administration time between the clients at the top of the list and those at the bottom of the list. You will find that 80 percent of your fees are coming from 20 percent of your clients. So why are you administering to that 80 percent when they represent a very small portion of your total revenue? They also represent a very large proportion of the costs of running your practice.

Some of the clients in this 80 percent majority could in fact be costing you money when you consider the cost of administering their requirements. And this administration time should include discussing fees and arguing about fees, discussing the excessive time spent because of the errors in their accounting records that have to be rectified every year. These are the same errors every year and due to the simple fact that they don't want to listen to your advice on how to fix the problem. They don't want to listen to your recommendations on changing to an accounting system that will overcome these issues and save them money. You can't help these people because they don't make use of those things on the side of their head (ears). And that is partly why the system works best when you introduce something new to your client base.

Let's look at a scenario here to clarify the situation:

You have decided that you no longer want to put up with wasting time asking clients for information. You are tired of chasing up lost bank statements and other information. So you have done some research and you have found a software package that will overcome these problems. The new system will save time with the client; time you are probably writing off in your work-in-progress because the client is not prepared to pay for it. In most cases they don't believe that their records are all that bad. And they will find it harder to believe if a relative (especially spouse) is responsible for these anomalies.

Think about it. Every year you have that same conversation with the client about the time your team spent rectifying the mistakes in the records. The client does not understand, and in most cases they don't want to understand. They can't see the errors and they can't imagine why you would take so long to complete the job and therefore cannot understand why you charge them so much. And you have in fact written off time on this job…every year and for too many years. No one is happy and the client can't see the value. Let's face it, very few clients appreciate the value of compliance and I don't blame them. It's a need, not a want. Here is another good reason to consider outsourcing compliance work to a competent and reliable bookkeeping service.

An accountant doing the crunch work...So many still do the crunch work. Good bookkeepers are far more efficient at this process.

So, you have found the accounting package that can resolve all these issues. The package allows the client to get their bank statement details fed directly into the system, which means no more lost bank statements and no more paper. The system is cloud based, which means the client will not lose any of their information. The system is easy to use, which means there are fewer anomalies. You will have access to the system online, which means that you don't have to attend the client's premises and you don't have to fiddle around downloading DVD's containing information that is generally full of anomalies.

The next step is to introduce this new accounting process to your clients. The best way to do this is to arrange a presentation and conduct a series of workshops so they can learn how the software works and also see the benefits that can be derived.

Make it easy for your clients to make the changeover. Offer to transfer all the information from their previous system as part of your package of services. Even do the changeover for free. Offer to throw the workshops in as well so that they will attend the workshops. It is not as if they are getting this for free. It is included in their accounting services package so they may as well take advantage of the services included in that package.

This is also a great opportunity to introduce fixed price contracts to the clients. Bundle up the services to include the transfer of all data across to the new system and all training workshops to assist with the implementation of the new system. While you are there, throw in unlimited meetings and phone calls. This is a great opportunity to kill two birds with one stone by introducing the new system of information gathering and including with it a new fixed price agreement setting out the fee for the client for the next 12 months along with the benefits that will be derived from the services shown in that fixed price agreement.

I would seriously consider throwing in the changeover to the new system for free. You will return this time five-fold with the time saved in not having to gather information or to repair anomalies.

And here is another great opportunity. Instead of just seeing your clients once a year to go over those boring financials and sign the tax returns, you could take this opportunity to express the benefits of preparing their accounts on a quarterly (or monthly) basis. Some examples could be:

➢ You no longer have to worry about compliance deadlines as we will take full responsibility for the lodgement of the Business Activity Statement (BAS) for the business, which means you can get on with your core business.

➢ If by some chance you receive a fine for late lodgement from the ATO, we will cover the fine, provided you have supplied the information to use by the requested date. Now this is taking out some of the risk for the client.

➢ We will discuss the progress of your business each month by checking the progress of your profit forecast and ensuring that we are on track to achieve your desired profit for the year.

- ➤ We can very quickly identify any issues that may significantly affect your profit as we are discussing your numbers on a regular basis.
- ➤ You will know exactly where you stand with the Australian Taxation Office (ATO).
- ➤ By preparing your BAS we can ensure that your GST is paid on time, which means no ATO fines.
- ➤ We will work with you to uncover opportunities within your business.
- ➤ We can monitor your key performance indicators on a more regular basis and make some recommendations that will improve your bottom line.
- ➤ We will work with you to determine the appropriate accounting package that will be best fit for your business. A system that will produce information to assist you with running your business, which means you can not only monitor progress accurately, the system will also save you time and money.

Can you see the opportunities here? When you transition your clients to the new software, you could include the preparation of a profit forecast (as opposed to calling it a budget) for the business for the next 12 months. You will enter this forecast onto their system, which means you can look at the variance between budget and actual each month to identify any material differences that need further investigation. This is the easy way to keep an eye on accuracy.

As part of your basic service offering you could include quarterly meetings with the client to discuss the progress of their profit forecast, which means you can ensure that the business is on track with revenue and profit targets. If your client does not want this minimum service and requests that you reduce the annual fee, I would recommend that you take this opportunity of placing this client in the ready-for-sale list, as this client will be better served by another accounting firm.

Look at this as an opportunity to talk to your client about things such as the key performance indicators for their business and how these can be monitored in order to improve the bottom line for their business; another opportunity to provide value-based advisory services for your client.

To summarise how it works:

- This is a great opportunity to transfer your clients to more functional software.

- This is an opportunity for you to cull clients that do not want to take advantage of fixed price agreements and your recommendations for transfer to a more functional accounting system.

- This process will provide an opportunity to introduce and offer value-based advisory services to your clients.

- You have the opportunity to prepare a profit forecast for your clients as a part of the minimum service offer.

TIP: This is an opportunity to inform clients of the way you are now doing business and also an opportunity to exit those clients who do not want to be a part of your new-look pro-active firm.

WHY IT WORKS

By transferring your clients to a system that gathers information efficiently you will overcome a major key frustration.

Think about the advantages of taking the time to sit down with your clients and preparing a profit forecast (or cash flow) for their business. The client will benefit by having a good hard look at the business with you and will have the opportunity to set some revenue and profit targets. In addition to that, they have the advantage of meeting with you to discuss any variations from that forecast that may be affecting profit goals. These variations may well be bought about by processing errors. The material variances on the variation report will expose these anomalies. This is not rocket science and is a very quick and efficient way to detect any errors on the client's file.

By preparing the cash flow forecast for the client, and checking the monthly variation report for material variations from the forecast, you are able to delegate more of the accounting process to trainee team members, or an outsource bookkeeping service. This also means that you can identify processing error very quickly, and, the best part, you are using your skills as an accountant to detect these anomalies.

Let me explain...

If the client has made a monumental error, it will stick out in the variation report and can be rectified immediately. The same goes for team members. The cash flow forecast provides a great reconciliation reference for the business, and with the new service offering you will be discussing the variance report at least once per quarter.

Why would you want to run your business any other way? And why would you want clients who don't want to come on board with this?

The other advantage is that every client is using the same accounting system and training is minimised. You can then standardise working papers and the firm will be far more productive. In fact, there will be more fees derived via the fixed price agreements and less time spent on the job. The client receives information in a timely manner and is now monitoring the progress of the business... a much better allocation of time.

This is a great elimination process. You may find at the conclusion of this process that you have culled all the clients you want to cull. Also, clients that show the initiative to take the new services on board are the type of clients that you want and will fit your definition of 'ideal client' even though they are outside that 80 percent of total fees. You can add value to these clients.

You can express the benefits to your clients and this will make it easier for the transition to fixed price contracts. The clients will see the value and will be prepared to invest more money with you when they can see the return from their investment in your services.

By having that meeting with the clients, you are providing a platform for a smooth transformation process. You see, by having that meeting with the client they are telling you that they don't want to change the way they do business with you. And because of this, these clients do not fit in with your definition of ideal client and should be transferred to an accounting firm that can better suit their needs.

You have now set the stage to transfer these clients to another accounting firm. You can send them a very polite letter that basically says that they have indicated to you in a recent meeting that they do not want to do 'this' and they do not want to do 'that.' And furthermore, you totally understand where they are coming from. Then you can inform them that you have gone to the trouble of finding another accounting firm that can better suit their needs. The correspondence will make sense to them because they can relate back to the meeting that you recently had with them, and will likely agree that it is time for them to move on to another accountant. In addition to that, you have even gone to the trouble of finding them another accountant who can better suit their needs, which means *they* don't have to go through this process.

By using this process of elimination you are not just sacking your clients. You have the opportunity to meet with them and determine which clients want to move forward with you. Those clients that don't wish to move forward are placed in, what I term, the clearance bin until you have finished the process. Then you can look for a business agent who can sell the client base to another accounting firm that can better fit in with the needs and wants of the clients. And let's not forget the proceeds from the sale of this block of fees.

To summarise why it works:

- At the end of the process you will have fewer clients, which means less administration.

- With the introduction of fixed price contracts you will increase your average fee per client.

- With the new accounting software you will free up valuable time to spend more valuable time with your clients.

- You will have more time to attract more clients of the type that you want.

- You will receive quality referrals from your clients.

- Your client retention ratio will increase dramatically.

- You will have more control over your client's affairs.

- You will be less stressed.

- You will receive some remuneration from the clients that you sell off (clients that no longer fit in with the way you do business).

- Same team members, more effective.

- No more timesheets, more efficiency and more profit.

- You have the opportunity to look at doing some value pricing proposals with your clients.

TIP: You need to be clear with your clients and let them know the way that your practice does business.

THE BENEFITS

Administration is the biggest killer in an accounting practice. You don't make money from it, but you sure can lose plenty of money by not doing it. By applying the Pareto Rule to your accounting practice you will reduce administration time by up to 80 percent. You will free up valuable time so you can spend more time with your clients and provide more valuable services that they can really benefit from.

Your clients will be happy. These are the clients that have been up the front of the aeroplane begging for your attention and you keep walking past them to go to the back of the aeroplane where there are more clients, fewer fees and more noise (and more administration). You will now be spending time with the clients at the front of the plane.

You have the opportunity to cull the clients that are causing all the problems in the organisation, the ones who cause all the stress and the ones that make your good team members leave.

You will eliminate the frustration of gathering information; the biggest time waster for knowledge workers. You have now introduced a more efficient system that eliminates this frustration.

You will eliminate arguing with clients over fees. They now have fixed price agreements that are prepared before the work is commenced. This is much better than the current situation where you do all the work, incur all the expense, spend all the time, only to find that the client is not happy with the amount on the invoice. This is all eliminated when you do the deal before the deal, get the money out of the way first, and demonstrate the benefits to the client.

Fixed price agreements give you the opportunity to discuss some value pricing with your clients and an opportunity for you to bundle services to demonstrate value to the client. There is also an opportunity for the client to express how happy they are to pay for these services as these services result in an increase in profit for their business.

The value of the service (from the client's perspective) before the project is commenced is often more than you ever had in mind. This means that you will not be leaving so much money on the table. I mean…provided you deliver the service, your client is hardly going to complain about a fee that they themselves suggested. The client determines the fee based on the return on their investment in your accounting services. If you are assisting your client to make more profit, they don't mind sharing some of that additional profit with you because in reality you are not costing them any money. In time, the accounting fee will be a very low percentage of the increase in bottom line profits that the client will be generating.

You will free up valuable time in your business. You will no longer be dealing with unreasonable clients, those clients that annoy the hell out of you and your team members and cause a heap of stress. Let them go. And if you play your cards right you will be able to sell these clients and put some money back into the business that could be applied to some incentives for the team members, a new office fit out etc.

To summarise the benefits:

- Fewer clients by number.

- Less administration - reduced by up to 80 percent.

- More time, more space.

- Fewer complaints.

- No more winging clients.

- No more stress with unreasonable clients.

- An increase in the average value per client.

- More time to discuss more clients.

- More referrals from your existing client base.

- More time to prospect for more clients of the type you want.

- You will know where you stand with your client base.

- You can start doing business the way you want to do business.

- Your clients receiving a great return on their investment in your accounting services.

- Retention of valuable clients.

- Retention of valuable team members.

- You can put some money back into the business from the sale of these clients.

TIP: You need to purge your client base every three years to ensure that you free up valuable time to give awesome service to your valued clients.

CASE STUDIES

We were engaged by a three-partner accounting firm to assist with improving their productivity. We did a quick tour of the workplace and had a brainstorming session with the team members, including the managers, and made the following observations:

➢ There were hold ups in the system associated with the gathering of information from clients.

➢ The firm did not have a system to ensure that all information, needed to complete the job, was gathered from clients before commencing the work.

➢ There were consistent anomalies in the information received from the clients and these same anomalies had to be rectified by team members year after year.

➢ There were a number of different accounting software packages being used by the clients and this meant the firm received information from their clients in all shapes and sizes.

➢ The same clients were making the same mistakes each year with their record keeping.

➢ The same clients each year were putting pressure on compliance deadlines.

➢ The firm provided a training program for their clients in order to reduce the error rate in the information they provided. Very few of the clients attended these workshops, probably because they were put on for free.

- ➢ Even where clients engaged a bookkeeper to prepare their accounting records there was still a high error rate.
- ➢ A number of the clients would continually complain about fees.
- ➢ The work-in-progress write-off was too high.
- ➢ There were a number of write-offs from invoices throughout the year as clients had complained to partners about the fee, and the partners buckled in on the argument in order to retain the clients. (That never made sense to me. I would have upped the ante on the invoice to get rid of the client).

When we met with the partners of the firm we found that the business was all over the shop. They had some fixed price agreements with clients, but the majority of clients were on time billing. There was no formal menu of services, and the fixed price contracts were not very affective as the partners still charged for some services on a time basis. The turnover of the firm was in excess of $2.5m and there were 13 employees.

The partners were stressed. There had also been a number of clients leaving the firm for a number of reasons, the main one being that fees were too high for what they perceived to be very little service. The defection of the clients was of major concern.

The partners had the opportunity to kill a number of birds with one stone here. Initially, they had to fix the information gathering problem. To do this they had to standardise the way they received information from their clients. My recommendation was that they transfer their small to medium size clients to Xero Accounting Software. With this cloud-based software, the client would receive all bank statement transactions directly into the accounting system and all they have to do is code the transactions. This means there is far less margin for error.

The other great feature is that the accountant has easy access to the information as the system is cloud based. And being cloud based means there is no loss of information and the information can be viewed from anywhere in the world, providing there is internet access. The advantage of the accountant having access to the system is that they can make any adjustments directly into the system. The point of the exercise is that we streamlined the way information was being gathered as everything was standardised.

The partners decided to conduct weekly workshops for their clients in order to show the benefits of changing their accounting system over to the new software package. To get the ball rolling they threw a party (which is about the only thing accounting clients will attend and normally only for the free grog) to announce the good news about the new software options. This would go a long way to eliminating arguments about continually having to fix anomalies in their records.

The next item on the agenda was to convert all clients from time billing to fixed price contracts and the goal was to phase out the time cost system within 12 months. When we conducted the Cost of Time Cost exercise we calculated that their time cost system was costing them $450,000 per annum in real terms, over 18 percent of gross fees. This seemed like a good enough reason for them to give the timesheets the flick.

The transition to fixed pricing could be synchronised with the transition from their existing software to Xero. It was easy. All that needed to be done was to include the transfer over to Xero as part of the packaging of services using their new menu of services. This was also a great opportunity to fine tune the menu of services and to offer four standard service packages. Each package would include the transfer and set up for the new accounting software. The partners had to come to terms with the fact that some clients would be reluctant to move across to the new software. They had to work on the script to ensure a good conversion rate. And in the process of introducing the new look, more efficient outfit with the new software and fixed price contracts on offer, they had to get used to saying to the clients "this is the way we are doing business here now."

In order to ensure the best possible conversion rate, the partners and managers had to meet with every business owner client to discuss the benefits to them of coming on board with the new and more efficient way of doing things.

And now we come to the third part of the process…the purging of the client base. The first thing to do here was to determine the definition of 'the ideal client' for the firm. This means clients that the partners, managers, and team members wanted to deal with from day to day, and nice people that listened to advice and appreciated their service. The first process of elimination would be those clients that flatly refused to transfer over to Xero and also those that did not want a fixed price contract with the firm. The partners agreed that if the client did not want to transfer to the recommended software immediately, that would be acceptable, but refusal to go ahead with both new software and the fixed price contract was unacceptable. The partners put some scripts together to ensure that the clients could understand all the benefits from transitioning to the new and more effective way of doing things.

In those instances where the client was providing accurate information, the issue of new software was recommended but not compulsory. These clients were not contributing to the information gathering problem.

The partners decided that they would not continue with any client that did not want a fixed price agreement. They discussed some options for these clients. I recommended that they keep these clients in a holding pattern until we had finished the purging process. In the meantime, they may change their mind about the proposal for fixed price contracts and changing software. And besides that, why would you just sack the client? Why not find the client another accounting firm that can better look after their needs? You do owe that to the client.

Then we came to the purging process. The partners prepared a listing of the client base. The clients were put in order of highest fees to lowest fees. The fee listing totalled around $2.5 million. In order to start the purging process we were going to apply the Pareto Rule to determine the clients that were contributing to 80% of revenue.

We drew a line on the client list at the point where 80% of the fees had been accumulated. And, you guessed it, there were just over 20% of the clients contributing 80% of total fees derived by the firm.

We then had to look at the clients above the line to see if they came under the definition of 'ideal client.' If they did not, they would then be considered for transfer to another accounting firm.

We also looked under the line to see if there were any clients that should be retained as they had indicated that they wanted to take advantage of the business advisory services with a view to growing their business.

One of the provisos for an 'ideal client' was that the client had to be a nice person to deal with, a person that would respect their advice and could afford to pay their fees. The partners decided to go through the client list and eliminate all those clients that were not pleasant to deal with. They also mentioned the clients that continually complained and argued about their fees. I recommended that they retain these clients for now and discuss fixed price agreements with these clients and show the benefits for them in doing so. If the client did not want to go with the fixed price agreement, then they would be sold. I suggested to the partners that all team members should have their say about which of the clients are not very pleasant to deal with as some clients would put on a pretty face for the partners and managers and put on an ugly face for the team members at the front line. We needed to get rid of these clients as well.

All they do is create stress and are generally responsible for good team members resigning.

We had a meeting with all the team members to determine the clients that they found to be unpleasant to deal with. I explained to the team members that there was no reason for them to be treated poorly by clients, irrespective of how much they were paying for the service. If the clients were just not nice people, they had to go into the clearance bin for sale.

The team members were delighted with the prospect of removing these clients and were very open and enthusiastic. The other great result was that they felt they were being empowered in this decision-making process and also felt some ownership of the process. The posture amongst the team members changed for the better.

The partners looked at the list of clients that did not fit the definition of 'ideal client' and they took on board the feedback from the team members. These clients were eliminated from the list of clients. Some were from above the 80% line. This meant that the line representing 80% of fees would be adjusted. Again we had to look under the line to identify any clients that indicated that they would be taking advantage of the client advisory services going forward.

During the interview process there were a number of clients that indicated they were not aware of all the services that the firm had to offer. These services were identified from going over the new menu of services. This was a great opportunity for the partners and mangers to find out the needs and wants of their clients and to bundle a number of services into their fixed price agreements. The service offerings included all meetings and phone calls. This meant that the clients could not really compare the fee for the new service to the fee that they paid in the previous year(s). Another interesting fact was that the majority of the clients that had previously complained about fees were happy to convert to fixed price contracts.

Every client that agreed to go forward with fixed price contracts would be paying more fees under the contracts. They indicated to the partners that the menu of services and the packages gave some clarity to the benefits to them of going down this path. And they could see the value in not having to worry about the time clock ticking when they were having a meeting or phone conversation with a partner or team member.

Most of the clients agreed that the transition to Xero would benefit them and they perceived that it was costing them nothing to do so, as this process was included in the entire package. They could also see they would not have to worry about the transfer of information onto the new system as this was included in their fixed price package.

The long and short of the process:

- ✓ Just over 75 percent of the client base was removed from the firm. The number of clients was reduced from 1,800 to 450.
- ✓ The reduced number of clients meant that there was more useable room created in the office.
- ✓ Administration time was reduced.
- ✓ Productivity levels increased.
- ✓ The remaining clients represented a fee base of $1,950,000 (just under 78 percent of the original fees generated).
- ✓ The partners successfully negotiated fixed price agreements with the remaining 450 client population. They also negotiated fee increases that averaged just over 24 percent as the clients were now aware of all the service offerings available to them. The bundling of these services also helped with the smooth transition.
- ✓ The partners were able to free up valuable time to spend with their clients to discuss advisory services.

- ✓ The partners also had more time to spend face to face with their clients, which meant their clients appreciated the value of this attention and showed their appreciation by referring more clients to them.
- ✓ The fee base from the new look client base was just over $2.4m, about $100,000 less than before they started the purging process.
- ✓ The average fee per client increased from $1,350 to $5,300.
- ✓ The clients that did not qualify to come on board were sent a very polite letter stating that it was obvious from recent discussions that the firm could no longer meet with their needs and wants, and further, that the firm had gone to the trouble of selecting another accounting firm that could better serve their needs and requirements.
- ✓ The partners agreed to sell the client base for 65c in the dollar. This was much less than the going rate of $1 in the dollar but they sold it on the basis that there would be no claw back clause and the settlement would be full and final. This meant there would be no come back and the partners would not have to waste any time dealing with issues that may arise from the sale of this client base. This meant they could focus on their core business.
- ✓ The firm derived just over $250,000 from the sale of the client base. They invoiced the clients upon transfer and wiped out any work-in-progress. They derived an additional $40,000 from this process.
- ✓ The remaining clients were invoiced prior to the commencement of their fixed price agreements. This exercise produced over $350,000 in revenue and wiped out the remaining work-in-progress. These fees were all negotiated and paid within 30 days.
- ✓ The proceeds from this exercise totalled $640,000.

- ✓ And what did the partners do with the proceeds from the client base? They had a meeting with the team members and decided to move into new premises. And they still had some change left over from the move.
- ✓ All clients were on fixed price agreements (or change orders for any work outside the scope of the FPA).
- ✓ The firm eliminated timesheets in less than 12 months.
- ✓ The productivity went through the roof.
- ✓ There were no more debtors to deal with.
- ✓ There were no more complaints about fees.
- ✓ All clients paid on either the first of the month or the 15th of the month. The only administrative task in relation to fees was to reconcile the fees received with the fixed price agreements. Normally the same fee each month.
- ✓ The firm no longer had cash flow issues caused by all their money being tied up in work-in-progress and debtors.
- ✓ They saved over $450,000 per annum by flicking their time cost system.
- ✓ Net profit ratio increased by more than 35 percent.
- ✓ No more stress.
- ✓ No more unpleasant clients.
- ✓ No more frustration with the gathering of data.
- ✓ With the new set-up the firm was able to easily outsource a vast majority of their compliance work to reliable bookkeeping services.
- ✓ The partners decided to purge the client base every two years.
- ✓ Client defection reduced to almost nil.
- ✓ Very few team members leaving.
- ✓ Referrals went through the roof.

Action Steps to Assist with the Implementation of these Strategies

- Conduct a Pareto Analysis on your client base to determine where most of your profit comes from.

- Define your 'ideal client'.

- Determine the way you want to do business.

- Determine how you are going to exit clients that do not fit your definition of 'ideal client'.

- Set the date for the next review of your client base.

- Involve all team members in the client reduction process.

Recommended Resources

"The 80/20 Principle"- Richard Koch

For more information about the Xero Accounting Systems visit the site:

www.xero.com

A Closing Note

I hope you enjoyed reading this book as much as I enjoyed writing it. This book bought back some fond memories of my professional past.

When you have implemented some of the strategies I would appreciate you sharing your success with me. You can do this by visiting the web site at:

www.newbusinessbreakthroughs.com.au

You could also send me an email…

peter@bizconnectionsaustralia.com.au

I would love to hear about your success.

Peter Lawson is the founder of the Biz Connections Group. He has more than 30 years experience in accounting and business consulting. Peter is a marketing architect, spending most of his time coaching accountants and bookkeepers how to offer marketing systems to their clients as part of their service offering. He is more of a strategic adviser than he is a coach, if that makes any sense.

After building a successful accounting practice, Peter partnered with a number of business clients and accounting firms and assisted them in successfully growing the business and improving the bottom line.

Peter's interest in business development started when he purchased a licence from Business Thinking Systems (BTS) back in 1997. Armed with the tools from BTS, Peter's first client was his own practice. Peter also attended a Results Corporation Boot Camp in 2000 as a continuation of his professional development of advisory services for his clients.

The business development unit within his practice quickly took over as the major source of revenue in the practice, out-gunning the compliance and tax division and the financial planning division.

During his 22 years in practice, Peter sold three very successful accounting practices that he started from scratch.

Peter is now sharing his secrets for success with the accountants and bookkeepers around the world.

For more details about the Biz Connections Group, visit our web site at:

www.newbusinessbreakthroughs.com.au

OTHER BOOKS

'Creative Cash Flow - 8 Innovative Business Strategies to Boost Profit' by Peter Lawson

I could best describe this book as business planning and consulting in motion. This book will take you on a journey through the business development process and a client that we turned around from the jaws of insolvency to a very profitable organisation that sold for more money than the owner could ever have imagined.

This book is available on Amazon:

www.amazon.com/dp/B00ALLR84Y/ref=rdr_kindle_ext_t mb

You can also purchase a paperback copy of the book through Amazon or from our web site at:

www.businessdevelopmentspecialists.com.au